AF411748

Dollbaby

Triumph Over Childhood Sexual Abuse

Linde Grace White, M.Ed.

Foreword by Robert A. Keefer, M.Div.
Princeton Theological Seminary

CEDAR HOUSE PUBLISHERS
MONROE, VIRGINIA

Published by Cedar House Publishers
P.O. Box 399
Monroe, VA 24574-0399
www.cedarhousepublishers.com

All Scripture quotations are from the Revised Standard Version of the Bible, copyright 1952 [2nd edition, 1971] by the Division of Christian Education of the National Council of the Churches of Christ in the United States of America. Used by permission. All rights reserved.

Cataloging-in-Publication Data:

White, Linde Grace.
   Dollbaby : triumph over childhood sexual abuse / Linde Grace White ; foreword by Robert A. Keefer.

   p. cm.
   ISBN: 978-0-9676289-5-0

1. Child sexual abuse—United States—Psychological aspects. 2. Sexually abused children—United States—Psychology. 3. Adult child sexual abuse victims—United States—Psychology. I. Keefer, Robert A. II. Title.

RC560.C46 W46 2005
362.76   2005927285

Printed in the United States of America
Cover design by Bruce DeRoos

For survivors of sexual abuse
and those people who help them recover themselves.
Love in action is the greatest healer.

Contents

Contents

Acknowledgments

To Carol for listening, midwifing, putting up with, encouraging, praying for, driving, handing out tissue and watching the dock for the ship to come in. Thanks for the burning ceremony and the use of the side of your house. You are an important person to me.

To Bob and Kathleen for their love, friendship and support. No way could there be this book without you. Thanks for the use of your fireplace and the side of your house.

To Linda, Marge, Jacqueline, Kathy, Rosemary, Jill, Blythe, Carol M., Carol S., Liz and Anna for reading my manuscript and still being willing to buy the book. I love you.

To Rob and Brad, my physicians, who didn't just say I was nuts when they met the alters, and the therapists who took on my case for teaching me things I needed to know, whether positive or negative.

To VOICES in Action, Inc. and, especially, Judy and Holly for printing my stuff, leading my recovery group and opening doors and windows to other survivors. Nobody is alone.

To David for reading and answering my letters and for putting me on the right track to discovery. I value the friendship you and Margaret have shown me.

To my children and grandchildren for continuing to love me and support me even though you probably won't be able to stand reading this book. I understand—it still hurts me, too.

Acknowledgments

To the courageous survivors of trauma, especially sexual abuse, who are becoming whole day by day. I hope my book helps you to persevere, heal and be your best self. I am a friend to you.

To Debbie and everyone at Cedar House. You made it possible.

Foreword

I am grateful for this book. As a pastor, a friend and a person who loves a really good story, I have benefited from *Dollbaby*. I am glad Linde Grace White is sharing her story with the world. I know many counselors, pastors and therapists will agree with me.

Although we are taught how to empathize with others, we know perfectly well there is nothing better than meeting someone who understands because that person has been in the same sort of place. I recall Miguel de Unamuno writing that the best moment in reading a book is suddenly to realize, "I have been this person!" This book is for anyone who has been Linde Grace.

We all probably know someone who has been Linde Grace. Now, you may not be aware that you know her or one of her millions of sisters (and brothers), but you do. One of the difficulties victims of sexual abuse have is overcoming dissociation; they experience the world not through their own eyes but through the eyes of alternate personalities they create to protect themselves. They rarely feel at home in their own bodies. While they are learning to reconnect with themselves, to live in their own bodies, we, their friends or families, find ourselves at sea when we try to understand them. This story will help you see the reality of your friend who has been Linde Grace.

For anyone who likes a good story, *Dollbaby* offers plenty. The most important element in a story is a character you can care about. The wonderful experience of this book is caring about a fractured person who struggles to care about herself and to become whole. Linde Grace is not the only character you will care about because all of the people in this story are complex, interesting and even a tad exasperating. Perhaps like the folks around the corner from you.

In Genesis 32, Jacob was pondering his difficult family relationships when God jumped him and wrestled with him all night. I keep trying to grab hold of God and wrestle because of the many ways evil manifests itself in the lives of people I care about. I wish God would give a good account of the divine stewardship of the world. From the Book of Job to my own work on the theology of sin, I don't find good explanations of why these things happen. They do happen, however, and a wrestling match with God seems like an important aspect of coming to terms with them. Linde Grace may resist being compared with Jacob, and well she should; unlike her, Jacob brought most of his trouble on himself. However, I appreciate that she neither simply submits to God nor rejects God, but decides she has to deal with God somehow. Jacob limps away from his wrestling match with a new identity, a blessing and a dislocated hip. Linde Grace likewise gets a new identity. Like Jacob, she may limp, but she receives her divine inheritance.

What will you and I take from Linde Grace's struggle? Renewed empathy, I hope, and better understanding. We also can learn something about abuse and abusers, and not only sexual abuse. Those who have suffered mistreatment—children, spouses, employees—will find some aspect of Linde Grace's story that helps them say, "I have been this person!" At the least, we care about someone who has been this person. A great gift we give ourselves is to care about Linde Grace.

Robert A. Keefer, M.Div.
Cincinnati, Ohio

Dollbaby

She's a pretty dolly, that me-shell,
Perfect curly hair, shiny clean,
Plastic blue eyes staring out,
Rolling back to see the blackness inside,
Permanently pink lips in a faint smile.
Little me, baby me, is way inside,
Peeking out, quivering stomach-sick,
Dizzy-crazed knowing assault is coming.
He doesn't know I'm in there.
A quaker in every sense, tense, watchful.
I've decided to live, not die,
So I'm the dollbaby—his dollbaby—
Warm, breathing, beautiful,
Entirely numb, floating far, far away.

One

Frustrated. Stuck. That's how I'm feeling as I lie down on the old, poorly refinished sleigh bed. I am in my upstairs apartment on Springfield Pike, stretching out on the pink quilt. It's early evening, in the spring, 1991. The days are longer now, windows can stay open in Cincinnati, Ohio, so the birds settling down for the night accompany me as I slip off my shoes. I am alone with the dog, Cleo, who is sleeping on the couch which he's been told ten thousand times to keep off. My children are out of the house. Laura has her own apartment in Clifton, fifteen minutes away; Jeff is in school in San Francisco; Karen is still living with me, but she's out for the night with her friends. They've grown up quickly.

For about six months, I've seen a therapist—David— every week, trying to figure out why I am so depressed. We seem to be getting nowhere, and it's costing a lot of money, which I can ill afford with two children in college and one in high school in a neighborhood where money means something. I am trying every means at my disposal to get this therapy over with. My physician has sent me to the psychiatrist who has prescribed antidepressants and says ten or twelve visits to the therapist will get me right back "in the pink," so to speak. Ha!

A few days earlier, in desperation, I had called a friend—another David—in Louisville to consult about my problem. That call has led directly to my current spot, reclining on my bed, with a notebook and pencil by my side. Louisville David is in private practice as a psychotherapist, but I know him because he taught my ex-husband in seminary. As a seminary wife, and as a pastor's wife, I got to study right along with my husband as he developed his own career as a pastoral counselor. Surprising? We both have plenty of skills. My master's degree is in guidance and counseling. In fact, these experiences in the world of education have helped me to know I have a problem to begin with. So, I know Louisville David will have an idea. His idea is what I'm currently trying out—autohypnosis.

I'm attempting to relax and breathe deeply. Louisville David says to put myself in a "light trance" in order to remember whatever it is that is disturbing me so much that I've lost interest in everything. I have recently divorced a second husband, I feel ashamed of the way I can't seem to handle relationships and I have begun simply not to care about much of anything. I'm breathing until I'm feeling lightheaded. My eyes are closed except for one quick look at the clock. I've decided to give this trance business about twenty minutes. At least I'll get a little rest, if not insight. It gets a little darker in the room, although it's hard to tell if that's because it's darker outside or if I'm starting to swirl into my brain.

I know in a few seconds that it's whirling inside that's going on because I lose the sense of my surroundings. I'm floating as if on a plastic raft in a pool, just rocking with the motion. I feel my weight borne up by the mattress as I sink deeper into another kind of awareness. I'm barely conscious of the notebook at my side, but it's there because Louisville David says to write down, with my non-favored hand, whatever I experience. The use of the non-favored hand (in my case, left) is to allow the child in me to express herself. I'm having a peculiar dialogue in my head now. Part A says, "Write down that you feel heavy. Don't forget that you're starting to feel funny inside your underwear." Meanwhile, Part B is sniffling that she can't write. She doesn't know what Part A is talking about, and she doesn't like whatever's happening "down there."

I'm not seeing Part A or Part B, but I do know that I am experiencing being two people at once. At first I can't understand who these people are, but as I concentrate on how I'm feeling, it begins to clear up. Part A appears to be the adult person I am more or less familiar with. It's the me I usually inhabit and I am watching events without so much seeing them as feeling them. I'm sensing a frightening claustrophobia as if I am going to be crushed and there is no way to move. I can't roll or push away whatever it is. And I can't scream, even though I want to. I'm gagging instead. Something is in my mouth and crammed down my throat. At the same time, sexual arousal (this information comes courtesy of Part A) is increasing. Part B is wishing she could die or anything to get away. She's appealing to Part A for help in knowing what to do.

Part A is asking questions of the situation. Part A is acutely sensitive to Part B's feelings, but, for a while, just can't grasp what is taking place. Then it dawns on Part A—"Daddy is doing this! Yeah. Daddy is poking his—ooh, yuck!" Both Parts A and B are nauseous. Part A calls a halt to the whole autohypnosis experiment—right now!

I come back into the room and try to write what I've

experienced. This is a no-go. The writing is gibberish, and I try to guess why. I relive the trance, but now I'm analyzing, being the journalist, getting the who, what, where, when and why. Okay. Daddy is holding me down. He's putting his penis in my mouth. That explains why Part B can't scream. I'm at home in Louisville where I was born, and I haven't had my second birthday yet. That's why I can't write and that's why I don't know what to say. I'm too little, and I don't have any vocabulary for sexual abuse.

Well, I'm not frustrated any more. Shocked, flabbergasted, sick to my stomach, dizzy, confused—yes, but I'm not stuck. I ponder what to do. I don't know what to do. I have to wonder if this is real or if I've just made up some fantastic story. I like to write stories, but I've never had any ideas like this. I decide to call Therapist David, and see what he says.

I sit on the side of the bed for a few minutes, collecting my wits. Cleo ambles in, and studies me with those big basset hound eyes, ears hanging almost to the floor. He stinks, a good thing because it jars me into the present. I head for the kitchen and get both of us a drink of water. I'm astounded that mine goes down. Then, I call and leave a message with David's answering service. They're still using real people at this time, so I don't have to wade through a menu of press one for this and two for that.

While I'm waiting for David to call back, I wander through the apartment. Karen and I have been living here on the second floor of a Victorian house for less than a year. The landlady lives downstairs with her husband and their baby. I'm old enough to be her mother. The rooms in the apartment are large. We have a fireplace, but it doesn't work. Karen has her room at the back, the space taken up mainly by the waterbed she insisted upon having. We have had to show the landlady our insurance policy covering damages by the waterbed before it is okayed. Karen is also responsible for our owning the dog. She chooses a basset hound because she's found out that the landlady had a basset she'd loved growing up. I'm so much a peace-at-any-price person that I give in to Karen on almost every issue. Maybe if she has a dog, I won't have to give her quite so much attention. Since I've divorced her father, she's been demanding more of me emotionally than I am able to give. She really didn't like my second husband at all—none of the children did—and ultimately, I realized, too, that even in his forties, he needed his mother. The major emotion I can feel is depression, dark, deadly, and deteriorating me rapidly like a fast growing cancer.

When the phone rings, I jump. It's like the voice of God out of the burning bush. I pick up, and it's David.

"Something funny just happened," I say, after the preliminaries. "I tried putting myself in a trance." I go on to describe what happened.

"Sounds like you had a flashback," he tells me.

"A what?" It isn't that I don't know what he's talking about, it's that I still can't believe it. I want him to tell me I'm crazy or hallucinating, that I should get right down to the hospital and have them sedate me. I'd rather be crazy than abused, I think.

In the end, he says I should try to calm down, make notes, and we'll talk about it at the next session. He wants to know if I'm okay alone. I guess so. I feel no urges to hurt myself. I'm still kind of numb. Since it's a Friday night, I don't have to teach the next day, so it doesn't matter very much whether I sleep or not. I have some painkillers left over from some dental work. They usually knock me out, so I figure I can take one later.

After I hang up, I get Cleo's lead. He is so excited I can hardly get it snapped to his collar. I grab a couple of plastic bags and my keys; we set out for the evening walk. While we're walking, I get that eerie sense of not being present. There I am, on the sidewalk, with a living, breathing animal at the other end of a piece of leather, and I don't really know where I am. I am in my neighborhood where I've lived for sixteen years in various houses, and I don't know where Cleo is taking me. He is meandering down the sidewalk, sniffing, sniffing, sniffing, finding I-don't-know-what to interest him. He's checking out squirrel paths, the other dogs that have been walked here, places where cats are prowling, mice, birds, where the mailman cut through the yard. I'm hardly aware of whose house we're passing, tripping over irregularities in the sidewalk I've known were there for years. I can't stop my mind from going back to the scene in the bedroom.

Until this evening, I'd thought I was pretty normal.

For Your Convenience

For your convenience, I am a girl.
For your convenience, I am cute,
Little,
Ignorant,
Adore you because I know nothing else,
And live in your house under your authority.

I do remember the pain, the gasping for breath,
My mouth stuffed with body parts
I shouldn't have known you had.
I remember shrinking,
Shrinking into a box I gave a name to,
Hiding myself from reality, knowing I never mattered,
Except for your convenience.

Two

Outrageous! That's all I can think. I'm wallowing in disbelief like a hog in mud. All the times Therapist David has said, "That's unusual. Most people don't have that experience," come back in a jumble of information. I've been babbling to him about my childhood for months, never connecting his comments to whatever I was saying. It didn't seem odd to me that I didn't have a door on my bedroom until I was in my teens. Family members wandered in and out of the bathroom while I was using it on a daily basis, usually without knocking, just singing out "I'm coming in to ..." whatever. That kind of thing seems to have been inappropriate. Surprise!

My therapy sessions take on a different character. I don't remember sexual abuse all at once. Far from it. I'm in an unexplored wilderness. I could be at the North Pole or the jungles of South America for what I know about the issues. Innocent childhood memories and experiences take on a suspicious and sinister nature. I realize I really don't remember much about being a child—perhaps because I was never a child to begin with. It's several years into therapy before I come to terms with the fact that I was preverbal when the abuse began. I really don't know any words for it.

One incident does roll into my befuddled thinking system, and that one stands as a symbol for many similar events. Daddy has taken me on a "date." He takes me on dates often, sometimes to run errands with him, but usually the two of us are just out to get a Green River or a chocolate soda at Grant's Drug Store up the road from our house.

I am dangling my legs over the front passenger seat of the old Plymouth. Daddy likes Plymouths, and that's what he always gets when we need a new car, which isn't often. It's summer, I know, because I'm wearing some little green shorts my mother made and a halter top to match. I have on sandals, even though Mom is perpetually exercised over the possibility of injury to my feet. We're driving along, and I say (to Daddy's intense amusement), "I bet when people see me riding up front with you they think I'm your wife, only little." "Well, maybe they do," he chortles before changing the subject. He talks about things he thinks will interest me, but they are so funny to him that he can't keep a straight face.

"Who are you today?" he asks every night when he gets home from work. I give an involved answer because I have spent the day playing with my doll, Betty Ann. I am, besides Betty Ann's mother, an actress, model, secretary or something. I see no problem whatever with having my baby at work all day with me, and I get to work at home among an array of child-sized furniture, mostly of the kitchen and bedroom variety. I give myself a different name every day. When it's almost time for Daddy to get home, Mom and I fix up. We put on clean clothes if we need to and, the best part, make up. The Avon lady regularly visits and gives me a sample tube of the lipstick shade they are currently promoting. Mom lets me apply it every afternoon because we want "to be pretty for Daddy."

What I slowly discover, as I think back, is that Daddy, after he pecks Mom on the cheek and tells her the highlights of the day, devotes all his attention to me. What I remember is being taken to my parents' bedroom where Daddy and I lay on the big double bed and play games. There are whispering games and tickling games, then the games I've blocked out. I know this is true because Mom has time to cook supper while Daddy plays with me. My older brother is running around the neighborhood someplace. At least, he isn't home. Since the time frame is the late '40s and early '50s, I realize now that Mom wasn't using any convenience foods, had no toaster oven or microwave, so cooking supper took at least an hour unless she'd been cooking soup or stew all afternoon.

I am so tired after the games that I can hardly sit on the white backless stool that is my chair for supper. Our kitchen is large by the standards of the day, but it barely holds the four of us. The table is a drop leaf and most of the time, Mom only opens the one leaf that isn't next to the wall. There is an oil-cloth tablecloth on it. My brother sits on the end near the refrigerator and Daddy sits opposite him with his back to the back door. Mom and I sit on the side. Ever since I could sit up at the table, Mom has been making a big deal out of my using my right hand. I think, years later, that I am probably natural-ly left-handed, but she believes that left-handed children have a lot of trouble in school. My brother, though he is right-hand-ed, has some trouble in school already, but that's mainly because he's smarter than his teachers and doesn't mind a bit if they know it. The dinner problem is that I knock over my glass of milk almost every night and drop my fork as well. This is, of course, because I am clumsy with my right hand. I still tend to reach with my left hand and catch with my left.

The clumsiness is dealt with by everyone at the table yelling such comments as "She did it again!" or "Won't you ever learn?" and a lot tongue-clucking by my mother as she stops everything to get a rag to mop up. Craig, my brother, and Daddy laugh. I feel embarrassed and, often, leave the table for a while, ostensibly to use the bathroom in peace, but also just to get away. When I come back, I immediately go to my imaginary playmate. She is "Mary Lou," a little girl exactly like me in every way. She sits next to me, between me and Mom, on a stool like mine. Sometimes, Mom even has to set a place for her. The family believes I'm a very strange little girl, but that this reliance on the imaginary friend is the product of our living in a semi-rural area on a busy road where I have virtually no contact with other children. I actually have two friends—the aforementioned Mary Lou and a little boy called Tommy. I don't recall the content of our play, but Mary Lou and Tommy, my doll and teddy bears keep busy all day, and I have no idea I'm missing anything by not interacting with humans.

Besides berating me for clumsiness, my family also discusses Craig's almost daily wrong-doing. From Dad's point of view, Craig is the source of aggravation in his life. I can't think of any time in my life when I had the sense that our father even liked Craig, much less loved him or cared for him. Dad humiliated Craig at every opportunity, yelled at him and beat him on a fairly regular basis with his belt.

Craig, six years older than I, is a slightly built kid, blonde and blue-eyed. He looks like Mom's family. Dad, on the other hand, is a little over six feet tall, with a medium build, dark hair, blue eyes. He is, in fact, a fairly handsome man. He's strong because he does physical work every day, and, besides that, we have a half acre of property. In addition to the grass, we have a big vegetable garden and four fruit trees that normally fail to produce any fruit year after year. When he beats Craig, I can hear it from my bed across the hall—neither Craig nor I has a door. Mom sits on the top step and cries harder and harder as the beating progresses. Of course, Craig is screaming, and Dad is cursing, saying he isn't going to put up with whatever behavior is being punished. Meanwhile, I have crawled under my covers, shivering, cowing, feeling every blow, scared, wanting to stop it, powerless and hoping they'll forget they have a little girl. I never think it's fair.

A lot of Dad's anger seems to be triggered by the fact that Craig hates mowing the grass and working in the garden, but Dad drives him like a slave. Then, Dad complains that Craig doesn't take care of the tools and equipment right, not that Dad has ever really bothered to teach Craig how to do it. Once, only once, at Mom's insistence, Dad helped Craig fix his bike. Dad would have left it broken, but Mom made a big deal of it and said it wasn't Craig's fault the bike was broken (it wasn't).

Leland, my Dad, can fix just about anything. He has an extensive collection of machinery and tools in the basement and in the garage. He has jar upon jar of nuts, bolts, and nails. He also has a collection of pornography, but that's another memory I blocked. My cousin tells me she's seen it, and I do vaguely recall one instance where Dad showed me, I think, a calendar. I follow Dad around everywhere he goes. I hang out in the garden when he's working there, but he doesn't let me weed because I can't tell the difference between vegetables and weeds. I spend the winter evenings in the basement where he's working on some project or other. When I'm down there, I "dance" with the support poles to the old floor model radio we have. It has a record player in it. Daddy and I have "our songs" we listen and sing along to. While he's messing around at the workbench, I'm rubbing myself up against the poles and kissing them passionately. I'm pretending they are wonderfully handsome men who are absolutely entranced with me. I think Dad finds this entertaining. He puts on some records that purport to teach one Spanish conversation, and we practice saying stuff like "En el comidor, hay una mesa." "In the dining room, there is a table." A red book that goes along with the records shows the Spanish, the phonetic rendering and the English translation. I am not fluent in Spanish. He tells me all about the differences between Castillian Spanish and Mexican Spanish. Mexican is really not okay. Why he wants to know Spanish is beyond me. He has no command of English. Mom is always on him to correct his grammar, but it never happens. Until the day he dies, he persists in saying things like "has went." I believe he knows better, but continues his bad habits because it annoys my mother.

Elizabeth (Mom) is the first person in her family to graduate from high school. She is what we would today call "upwardly mobile," but it's not working out too well, especially since she's married to Leland, the son of second-generation German immigrants. No one seems to know where they came from, other than Germany, a big place, or why or how they got to Louisville. Many years later, Craig will research this at the Mormon Library in Salt Lake City, and come up with practically nothing. Leland is, as they say, "rough as a cob," referring to a rural practice of using dried corn cobs in the outhouse when the Sears Roebuck catalogue was used up.

Mom's large family (she's the fifth of eight, but has lost one sister to diphtheria) comes from Crab Orchard in eastern

Kentucky where they farmed. Changing fortunes on the farm has brought them to the city. Her paternal grandfather was an itinerant evangelist, so the family is strongly connected to the Christian Church. One of her older brothers is a minister, and the other one spikes the punch at Sunday School parties. Some of them form a band and go around singing at various churches in the country. Her brother-in-law, Turner, plays the jug, and her younger sister, Mary Belle, plays the guitar. She sings. The family lives a couple of blocks away from Leland's family in the west end of Louisville, close to Churchill Downs, not that any of them cares. Leland's sister, Mary Catherine, is Elizabeth's best friend. Their birthdays are about a week or ten days apart in April and they are exactly the same age.

Mary Catherine, whom I'm supposed to resemble, plays the piano every Sunday at the Evangelical and Reformed Church—St. James—and her whole family, including another brother, Marion (or Jim, as he became in California), and a sister, Bessie, belong. In 1929, Bessie is married and has a little girl of her own. For some reason I don't know, Bessie has moved back home. Mary Catherine and Leland are in their teens, so Mom knows Dad, too. When she goes to Mary Catherine's after school, Mary Catherine's mother unlocks the pantry to give the kids a snack. This strikes Mom as peculiar. Still, as number sixteen of seventeen children, Grandma is accustomed to a certain amount of regulation.

As I think back over what I know about my past and my parents' pasts, I become further convinced that Dad was simply a pervert from the word go and I do not understand at all why Mom married him. It's possible, I guess, that he sexually used her as a teen, then she felt she had to marry him, but I don't know for sure. That's a supposition.

If You Knew

Would you love me if you knew, really knew?
Mostly, it's not as bad as I think.
You're tolerant, huh?
Perhaps these pulsing, pus-filled sores
I see, smell, and feel
Look only like the faint pink traces of angel kisses
From where you are.

—————————— Three ——————————

While I'm in therapy, I'm canvassing my relatives and everybody I know for information. I'm leaving no stone unturned. I feel embarrassed to realize I've been abused, molested, or incested or whatever, but Therapist David keeps telling me that I didn't do anything wrong. I'm a victim. For a while, I kind of like being a victim. "Oh, woe is me!" I whine to myself and David. "I am forever warped by this. It's so unfair! I don't know who I am!" It's a lot like solving a mystery or reading a suspense novel—I've got to get to the bottom of this thing! I've got to know "whodunnit." Although I actually know who, I just don't know why or how or what real effects this has had. But this explains everything, doesn't it? In a word, no.

I read everything I can find on the subject of incest. There is quite a little bit coming out. I don't know whether it's just the fact that I'm discovering some horrible things about myself—coming awake, as it were, to reality—or whether, all of a sudden, a lot of people are finding out about their pasts. Anyway, I read about twelve books or so before I'm satisfied that I know what I'm up against. I've had a love affair with books and reading since babyhood. Craig tells me there was a book in front of my nose on a pretty much constant basis, and he was dispatched to read to me any time Mom needed us out of her hair for a while. I could read before I went to school—a good thing as there was no kindergarten in the Jefferson County Schools when I was five. I went right on to first grade, not even turning six until mid-November.

I'm about the youngest kid in my class at Prestonia School. My mother has accompanied me to school the first day, but she doesn't drive, so I guess a neighbor must have taken us. Craig is a sixth or seventh grader in the same school, so he is required to pick me up at the end of the day and make sure I get on the bus and off at the right stop. He is not happy about this. I am wearing one of mother's many fashion creations, complete with a hair ribbon to match. It's a green or blue plaid cotton dress with puffy sleeves, white collar and cuffs. I have white socks and ugly brown oxford shoes which my mother insists are good for my feet. I hate them. I want to be wearing my black patent leather Sunday shoes. No way.

I get four nickels and a penny tied up in the corner of one of mother's white handkerchiefs. This is lunch money. She instructs me to be sure to bring the handkerchief home. I want a school bag like Craig has. I could put the handkerchief in there, but mother has decided that first graders do not require book bags, or anything else for that matter. I have no school supplies. She waits until I'm seated where the teacher wants me to sit in a wooden armchair desk with a drawer under the seat for the books I don't have. There is a cloak room to hang coats in, but who's got a coat on in Louisville on the day after Labor Day? That cloak room is a little scary to me because it's dark and I don't like dark places. Once I'm in the desk, she comes over and tells me she's leaving. She gives me a kiss and reminds me about the handkerchief and waiting for Craig after school. I don't like being that close to Mom. I don't really like her that much, but she is the only mother I know anything about, and little girls are supposed to love their mothers, right? In therapy, I start to understand some about why I'm not especially fond of my mother.

School is a wonderful place. I'm smarter than most of the kids in my class because I can read. In school, we do a lot of fun things that don't happen much at home. We churn butter in a glass jar then eat it on white bread. I have had the experience of squeezing the color into a plastic bag of margarine, but churning butter is a new one on me. At school, we take field trips. We all climb in a big yellow bus one day and go to see "Cinderella," which Disney has just released in cartoon format. Yucky things happen once in a while when some kid wets himself, or when the kid across the aisle from me throws up into the drawer of her desk. Eventually, we have papers and pencils and books to put in the drawer, and hers is full. Best of all, school is a place where I can let down my guard a little. It appears that no one is going to molest me there, or ridicule me or humiliate me the way Mom does.

Now with my reading and therapy, I'm learning something about humiliation. Mom regards Craig and me as possessions more than people. She says everything we do reflects on her, and that the folks we encounter in school or church or wherever are going to judge her by the way we behave. We have to be perfect in every way.

Mom is a health freak. She reads bowel movements like a gypsy reads tea leaves, and will use any means at her disposal to get them to conform to her high standards for consistency, color, frequency and so on. It is not unusual for her to interrogate possible bathroom felons, and demand to see the evidence of individual performance. Of course, I lie whenever possible. I do not report any illness or malaise, but she makes her rounds of my body like the quality control manager in a dairy. She decides by the look in my eyes—a variation on iridology where lights or lack of them in my eyes reveal my health status—what ailment requires her attention. I don't look at my mother much. Even when I have a serious case of scarlet fever, I pass out before I say I feel sick. I suddenly feel heavy and sleepy. My throat hurts, and I don't think I want supper. When the room gets dark and swims around at three in the afternoon, I think I'll lie down for a few minutes, even though I know what a dangerous move this is. I lie down and can't get up. I go away somewhere and when I wake up, Dr. Shaw has arrived. I am in the big maple double bed in Mom's and Dad's room, on Mom's side nearest the door, and I'm looking at the carved pineapple-shaped posters. Mom thinks Dr. Shaw is the greatest thinker of our time, the leading edge of medical knowledge, and whatever he says goes. I am scared silly of him. He has yet to let me off the medical hook, and the only positive thing about him is that he recommends ginger ale to bring down a fever. We never have ginger ale or any soft drinks around unless somebody is sick.

This time, Dr. Shaw acts like something's really wrong. He gives my mother a bunch of orders, including keeping me in bed and sending Craig somewhere else for a couple of weeks. He prescribes sulfa drugs. They are new on the market, and he thinks they'll help. I have scarlet fever he says. I certainly believe the fever part—I'm burning up.

Dad has to take Craig over to our Aunt Bertie's house where she lives with her husband, Uncle Turner, and Maw-Maw, her mother. While he might have welcomed the respite, Craig walks home the two miles or so after school at least once to see Mom. She remarks that it breaks her heart to see the poor little guy missing home so much. Meanwhile, she is caring for me with her usual enthusiasm for sick people. The schedule is rigorously enforced. I get the medicine, I get bathed, bowel movements scrutinized, food intake controlled, and I'm left alone the rest of the time. Mainly, I don't care because I hate the attention I do get. None of it is pleasant and, I learn, it is not nurturing. On the contrary, all my books describe this treatment as debasing and dehumanizing, but, as the child, I didn't know since I'd always been treated as an object.

I try to explain all this to David, but my actual fear of speaking the words required to express my utter terror of my mother as health caregiver stymie me. Eventually, he sort of understands. I, even at age forty-something, after marriage, after giving birth three times and dealing with mildly ill children, cannot bring myself to discuss nose drops, cough syrup, enemas, shots or anything else in those words.

"You won't even say the words," David marvels. That's correct, to a point. It isn't so much that I won't—I just can't. It appears to be a primitive human sense that if you say the word, that makes it so. For most of my life, I have slept facing the door with a small light on because I'm afraid one of my parents (and when I'm 40 they are both dead) will come into my room at night to do something to me. This fear is not groundless. Things like this happen: I am asleep, but wake up nauseous. I've got a stomach virus, apparently. When I throw up twice, Mom wakes up Dad and asks his opinion on whether or not she should give me an enema to stop the vomiting. Fortunately, for me, Dad doesn't want to be bothered, so he says, "No," and I'm off the hook this time. But when we visit some of Mom's friends whose little boy kicks me, hits me and pulls my hair until I go sit with the adults and complain of a belly-ache, I get a choice. Since we have to leave earlier than planned because of my complaining, my choice is an enema or suppository. I choose the latter. We had to stop at a drugstore, and I never even go to the bathroom when we are visiting after that. I learn never to draw attention to my physical state. Of course, my brother is with us and he gets to laugh and tease, mostly because he isn't the victim here.

On Saturday mornings, before hair-washing (more on that later), we go to Dr. Shaw's office. Yes, this happens about every week with few exceptions. Everybody's blood pressure has to be scrupulously monitored—everybody meaning Maw-Maw, Aunt Bertie and Mom. I am dragged along for the general sport and outing, but, of course, I can at any time be commanded to appear before the doctor. It goes like this: Dad is rarely available to drive the ladies and me to the great man's office, so Uncle Turner gets stuck with the job. But if he isn't able to chauffeur, we meet at one house or the other and call a cab.

Aunt Bertie, once Maw-Maw is settled in the back seat (heavy sigh): "I've been taking those pills, but they don't seem to be doing any good."

Mom, from other side of back seat: "Have you been eating right? Getting enough roughage?"

Maw-Maw (I am jammed in the middle between them): "He told me to take a spoonful of mineral oil every day, but sometimes I take Phospho-Soda."

Mom: "Well, you have to keep your bowels and your mind open, I always say."

Aunt Bertie: "Did you hear Elinor (my aunt from Indianapolis) tell about that man she and Vivian (Elinor's sister) know that had the colostomy? She told about it when she was down here two weeks ago." (There is always some hapless victim to discuss—sometimes they engage the cabbie if topics are scarce in the medical field).

Maw-Maw: "I didn't hear that. What's that about—colostomy?"

I am slipping away into Nancy, my alter personality. Aunt Bertie explains what she knows, which is not a great deal. There follows considerable speculation on the whys and wherefores of the cancer that caused the colostomy solution in the first place. No one in the car knows the man in question or anything other than what Elinor via Vivian has told them two weeks ago. Since this takes place over fifty years ago, the man's treatment definitely does not meet today's state-of-the-art medical artistry. Not a lot is known at that time about colorectal cancer or how to prevent or cure it, but it has to do with bowels, always a compelling subject in this family. I am both morbidly curious and sickened, and pretty much disappearing from the scene. Maw-Maw opens her purse and gives me a quarter to play with and, perhaps, spend at the drug store. I learn that, even though I think I'm invisible and observing from a distance, my body is really squashed between Maw-Maw, who smells of Johnson's Baby Powder and some peculiar "old lady" scent, and my mother, who also reeks of talcum powder, and wears more make up (but not as much as my Aunt Margaret).

We arrive at Dr. Shaw's where the waiting room is mobbed because he doesn't take appointments. Miss Dougherty, the nurse, has frizzy red hair, is fair and skinny and is in constant motion between her tiny table in the front and the office complex in the back. The office consists of a waiting room the size of our living room, containing about a dozen maple armchairs and two wrought-iron tables with ancient magazines, most of which Aunt Bertie subscribes to herself. A long, dark, narrow hall behind a door leads to a miniscule room where the doctor's impossibly crowded desk, a file cabinet and one extra chair fill up all but about two square feet of space. The examining room with its iron and glass cabinets, bent iron chairs and gurney-type table make me feel cold and nauseous with fear, no matter why I happen to be there. Beyond this room is a much smaller, perpetually dark room where the big fluoroscope machine stands ready to indicate what's amiss inside you.

The ladies sign in with Miss Dougherty and receive an estimate as to what time the doctor will see them. If it's a long time and there are no seats in the waiting room (usually somebody will snatch up a child so Maw-Maw can sit down), Mom and I walk up and down the block outside the office. We go down to the big Rexall Drug Store on the corner and check out the medicines and medical equipment on sale. Mom usually looks over the combination syringes, hot water bottles and vaporizers. She prices baby aspirin (nobody knows about Reye's Syndrome) or nose drops (mostly too expensive since salt water will usually do). Then we walk back to Dr. Shaw's. If it's my lucky day, I get to sit out in the waiting room under Miss Dougherty's watchful eye while the grown-ups cram themselves into the inner office to worry over their blood pressure, which probably rises twenty or thirty points just from the excitement. They ask a million questions, sometimes get a new prescription which we then have to take back down to the Rexall Store to have filled, and get their thrill of the week from the doctor's wonderful touch, general interest and infallible wisdom.

I dread Saturdays. Once we're home from Dr. Shaw's,

Mom washes my hair. She likes my hair long, although it never grows past the very top of my shoulders. Her hairdo of choice for me is a single row of sausage curls all around. To her, achieving this look is simple, or would be, if I didn't carry on so much. First I have to climb up on the kitchen counter, having taken off whatever top I have on. I lie on a towel. The counter is hard and cold, narrow and higher off the floor than I am tall. I know if I fall I'm going to get hurt. Mom pulls and tugs, scrubbing me raw with shampoo and water. She dumps glasses of water over my head as it hangs over the kitchen sink. They don't make hair conditioner in those days, so the hair gets tangled and knotted up. My mother cannot be accused of being incompetent in the cleaning department. Whether its bowels, hair or whatever is in between, it is thoroughly clean.

After towel drying me dizzy, she stands me between her knees, grips my middle and proceeds to comb out my hair. I cry, scream, yell for a haircut, complain I don't care if I'm pretty or not (Mom seems to think I want to be pretty at any cost) or whine, but I'm caught. It hurts. Tears are streaming down my face, but Mom is relentless. When my hair is combed to her satisfaction, she fills her mouth with bobby pins and starts wrapping chunks of hair around her fingers and pinning them as close to my skull as possible without my actually bleeding. When she's finished with the ten or twelve curls, I'm free to go, but no running lest the pins fall out. My hair is usually dry by bedtime, but I sleep in the bobby pins because my hair is very fine and the curl will drop out overnight otherwise. In the morning, before Sunday School (if Dad hasn't had to work that day), the second comb-out occurs. It's only slightly better than the first one, but, by God, I'm just about the cutest little girl anybody has ever laid eyes on. I'm not impressed.

We are members of St. James Evangelical and Reformed Church, the very same church Dad belonged to as a boy. Did he attend then? I have no idea. His sister played the piano, that's all I know. The family joins there after a Sunday School teacher at the Bennett Avenue Church of Christ informed my then three-year-old brother that he would be going straight to hell unless he believed in Jesus. Mom let them know her thoughts on the matter: no three-year-old needs to be threatened with hell for any reason (she has plenty of ammunition of her own, so interference from Satan is not required to keep her kids in line). Anyway, our family knows all about hell—we're living there.

By the time I'm born, my parents are involved with the church, which I think may have been within walking distance of our house on Lentz Avenue. Still, for all her concerns about Craig's eternal fate (which is, at this writing, still to be determined), she doesn't ask to have him baptized until after I am born. The E&R Church practices infant baptism, but the Church of Christ has believer baptism where the candidate needs to be at least eight or ten years old to renounce sin. Mom makes that spiritual decision on our behalf, and with a couple of my aunts for godparents or sponsors, Craig and I are baptized on the same day. He is six, and I am four months old. The story of my baptism never fails to include the information that I behaved very nicely until the choir began to sing. Then I screamed!

Just before my second birthday, we move out of the neighborhood of the church. We still attend as often as we can, but Dad works most Sundays, and Mom can't drive. I have, however, by the time I'm about eight or nine, managed to attend Sunday School enough consecutive weeks that I have qualified to receive a plaster of Paris lamb. I haven't earned the shepherd (Jesus in unpainted plaster of Paris), but I'm definitely up for the lamb. I don't get it. An oversight, no doubt, but Dad goes upstairs and demands a lamb for me when I sit in a pew crying. This is unusual—crying in the absence of physical pain. I hardly know what to make of it when the lamb emerges from Dad's pocket, but that doesn't encourage me to let my feelings be known in any other context.

For all occasions, and for attendance at Sunday School, I have to have the right clothes. So does Craig, but he also has to go to school, so he and Mom clash regularly about what she is going to buy for him to wear. She only dresses her "doll" in the homemade clothes. Elizabeth is an expert seamstress. She can mix and match dress patterns or make up her own. She makes some mother-daughter outfits for us, and all her own clothes. Sometimes, I get to choose a fabric or color, but most of the time, I wear what she puts on me. She makes all the choices for me, and nearly all my pictures are taken to show off one of these dresses.

Her choosing extends to how I feel as well. Mom informs me as to how I feel about things. She will intervene in Dad's activities with me only so far as to say, "Leland, at least let her wiggle." I will be gasping for air, trying to scream, wishing I could die, and he is holding me down on the floor, tickling me. I'm red in the face. They tell me I'm having fun. He hurts me. They say I'm not hurt, just being a brat. They say they love me, but they're killing me. I learn early on that the best thing to do is to go away when all this trauma is happening. I don't bother trying to express any feelings for a couple of reasons: first, I am totally confused about what feeling is what, and second, nobody responds to anything I do anyway unless it directly interferes with what they want to do. Craig is allowed to tape my hands behind my back and tease and tickle me on at least one occasion. I end up rolling over the rug, landing on the register along the side of the living room floor. I can't get my breath for yelling, crying and rolling. I believe I am going to die. Finally, when the noise level gets high enough—my screeching, Craig yelling and laughing—Mom steps to the kitchen door and says, "Turn her loose, Craig." I can scream "Mama" all I want, but she isn't going to do anything. I don't recall her even telling Craig not to play this way or to leave me alone. These horrible feelings start emerging during therapy sessions, and I am so frightened of them that it is literally a couple of years before I can even begin to sort them out.

My dolls become more and more real to me. I wish I were my doll, but even that is not very safe. My brother likes to get back at me for whatever he thinks I've done to harm him, so when he isn't allowed to hit me, he hits and kicks my dolls. This has almost the same effect. When I remember this in therapy, I get mad, but all I know how to do at that point is to sit in my car and pound the steering wheel before I leave the parking garage.

David says, "What would you like to do when you're mad?"

On this particular occasion, I have had a minor run-in with my least favorite librarian at the branch library in my neighborhood. "Trash the library," I answer. David wants me to elaborate, but the concept of expressing anger is so bizarre to me that I can only sort of picture what I might do. I start to explore my anger—just a little.

I enter into correspondence with several people about now—my cousin, Louisville David and Richard Foster, who has written a book called *Prayer*, which has upset me considerably.

I have been keeping a journal since 1981 when my marriage began to die, and I am now stepping up the journaling action. I join a VOICES group—Victims of Incest Can Emerge Survivors. I set up weekly appointments with the associate pastor of my church to discuss spiritual issues which are now looming large. Another pastor in the Presbytery has some expertise in what amounts to a version of hypnotism, so I see him a couple of times to explore some body memories and to get a handle on my spiritual state from a different perspective.

With Therapist David, I am exploring my nightmares which I chart on a 1-5 scale with 5 representing the worst. I am now learning, to my surprise, that I have dissociative disorder, meaning that I have "split off" into several personalities, each of whom appears under various circumstances to field problems and the other people I come in contact with. It scares me to be doing all this, but I am obsessed with ending my misery, discovering who I am and picking up the pieces of my life.

My children don't want to hear about any of this. They say that it's too painful for them to know what I've been through, but I am absolutely terrified that Dad may have abused them, too, while I was off in denial. I am comforted to find out that none of them remembers anything except feeling put off, a little frightened and happy that I didn't leave them to be babysat by my parents. Together, we can't come up with more than one or two times that the children were ever alone with my parents. They've stayed with their paternal grandparents for days at a time and loved every minute of it. What a relief! I can never stop being grateful for whatever it was that warned me to be so cautious with my children. I just knew from the beginning that my parenting style was not going to include most of the elements that characterized my own upbringing. I took college level courses in child psychology and child development to obtain my teaching certification and my counseling degree. Somehow, nothing I learned prompted flashbacks or enlightened me as to my own history, but it certainly gave me a game plan for being a parent. I can only explain my blindness to my own situation as the post-traumatic stress disorder and dissociation. I could not tolerate the information at that time.

I have only one hint during all this time that there's something not right about my family. My husband and I drive to Atlanta, Georgia, to attend a conference for several days. I am pretty sure it was the Transactional Analysis Conference, probably in 1972 or 1973. Among the work-shops/seminars I attend is one on working with parents who abuse children. On the way home, we talk.

Me: "I could never work with child abusers. I would get so mad. How could anyone ever deal with them?"

Herb: "Do you know anybody like that?"

Me: "No."

A conversation now revolves around childhood memories and so on, connecting things we've heard at the conference with our own experience. Re-parenting is currently being explored, for example. In the course of talking, I say, "Oh, I've had a lot of 'out of body' experiences."

Herb now wants details, but I am shut down immediately because I realize I don't know where I go or why. I just know I can do it, that I can observe from a distance, that I don't want to know any more about it. I get uncomfortable talking about it, and I think Herb doesn't know enough himself to know anything to say or do to help me. The highway stretches out, dark and cold, I stare out the window at the oncoming traffic like a shiny string of beads, and change the subject to how soon we will get to Louisville to pick up our children at his mother's house.

Years later, going through pictures for an album for my son who married that summer, I discover a snapshot of my daughter at about age two or three in bed with my Dad one Saturday. After the initial horror, I realize that I was there. My child had run into Dad's room with me right behind her to "wake up Grampsie." As I am ordering the baby out of Dad's bed, Mom enters with the camera and snaps the picture. I'm the only one who seems bothered by this at all. My parents think it's "cute."

The nightmares seem to revolve around situations where I am helpless, and usually can't breathe. A lot of dead little girls appear in them as well. I write accounts of them in my journal in addition to making the chart to share with Therapist David. Any dream I remember long enough to write down is extremely complicated, detailed, colorful and upsetting. None of the accounts here actually gives all the information I got, but only what I could get written down.

(2:30 a.m.) Really scary nightmares about children dying. I am in a room (cabin?) with families on vacation. Somehow children wander out to a ditch where I can hear them screaming and see them kind of bobbing up and down. They are being killed and I can't help them. I dream the whole thing two times and wake up disoriented for a few seconds and terrified. I know I should help those children—I want to—but somehow I can't. Two images stand out: a child screaming from atop a young man's shoulder in a ditch—when I run there to grab child, they disappear— and a little girl sitting on a grave (fresh) and saying, "I'll die, too. This is mine." The others are children's graves. I try to save child in ditch and when I'm back, child on grave is gone—I know she's been killed. I am still scared. What can I do to get settled and go back to sleep?

In another, I am visiting my sister and brother-in-law (Herb's sister). They have small children. The house is one of the manses I used to live in. Almost every room in the house is so small that you are literally wedged into it, but the house is big—a lot of small rooms. Doors are pieces of wallpapered drywall maybe six to eight inches wide. I am so claustrophobic, but I say nothing. I have several scary experiences, a couple of them in bathrooms. Suddenly, I'm outside in some snow and I am cleaning the yard by wiping off the snow (surface only) with a bucket of H_2O and a sponge—this is freezing into a sheet of ice. The children come out on a window sill to talk to me—they are in p.j.s. The man has leaned out another window to say something to me. The kids are mimicking him when the middle child, a girl of about four, slips out the window. She is hanging by her arms on the slippery window. She is facing me with her hands holding on above her head. She is quiet. I am screaming for help and hoping I can catch her if she falls. The man finally appears and lifts her inside. I look around the yard. I go inside—I am trying to find a bathroom that isn't cramped and small. I meet the middle girl in the hall. I am pushing my way frantically out of one of these tiny rooms. We can't both fit in the hall. She wants me to come play in her room. I am too scared. I've got to find a bigger room.

In another dream, a little girl has died and I am at the cemetery. I see my Dad in his wheelchair looking very sick. When I speak to him, he says something rude, then falls out of the chair. I feel disapproved of because the people around blame me for upsetting him, but would also be angry if I didn't speak to him. My journal has pages of analysis of these and many other dreams, but it all boils down to my attempts to make some sense out of my childhood. The littlest girl inside, Linnie, is trying to learn to trust me, and through the dreams, she is sharing her fear, terror, wish for death and decision to live. I am constantly feeling the pain of this child. I feel "little," so I talk less to people and stay out of groups because I'm afraid of embarrassing myself with some four-year-old observation.

Persistence in these various avenues of resources pays off. Although Craig thinks I've thoroughly gone off my rocker, he is willing to provide information to me. He doesn't catch on to why I want to relive all this grim and ugly stuff, why I'm willing to suffer so much pain. Sometimes I wonder myself. His wife, Rosemary, and his daughter, Jill, are highly supportive of me. They give me their perspectives and experiences with my parents. Even my ex-husband shares his impressions of my dad when I finally think to ask him about it.

My niece tells me about times when Mom openly favored her brother over her, how critical Mom was of a five-year-old's efforts to help set the table. Jill talks about being afraid of her grandparents. Herb says he always thought my dad was "a dirty old man."

I hurt so much and I am so angry that I take field trips to try to manage things. I take the two-hour trip to Louisville by myself to stand in front of the mausoleum where my parents are interred just so I can tell them what I really think. I write a letter to Dad. I go to a friend's house and throw water balloons at the brick wall because I live in an apartment complex, and I know my neighbors wouldn't understand. I have to do this more than once. I make little penises out of clay at school where I'm teaching, tear them apart, then wad up the clay and start over. When I think I'm able, I take paper and write down the notions and thoughts I'm ready to let go of and burn them in a friend's fireplace or in a little outdoor ceremony on another friend's sidewalk. I get a $3 pass to the county parks and hike until I drop and the dog's worn out. I pound out tunes on the piano because this has been the only way I could express feelings as a youngster. I pick out my own "Top Ten" hymns and play them over and over. I talk and talk until I'm getting sick of it myself. And I research my past.

Tapestry

A raveled tapestry is my Self,
A tangled weave unwoven
Of colors, textures, space, and knots,
Few threads remain unbroken.

The warp and weft were skewed
And no clear pattern laid
Before the master weaver left
It all to a deceitful maid.

So now I have to weave my Self,
First charting out the plan,
Then working out the tangles
And straightening each strand.

Only then can I, unlearned
In the weaving art,
Begin to make a masterpiece
From a shattered, broken heart.

Four

I begin my research with the major offender. My dad died in 1984 at the age of seventy to no one's especial dismay. We had had ten years of unmitigated problems with him. Mom had been killed in an automobile accident in 1973, and the worst of Dad almost instantly emerged. I hardly know where to start now that I have remembered the abuse, but I go to my relatives first. Perhaps I've misinterpreted—yeah, that's the ticket! Somebody is going to set me straight in a New York minute. But, no. My relatives on both sides of the family respond with nothing but support. They are sure sorry I remember all this. They wouldn't have mentioned it, but since I brought it up. ...

Craig's response is "Goddamnit." I gather from this that he doesn't disagree that the abuse happened, he has simply been hoping I had forgotten. Aunt Margaret, who was briefly married to Dad after he was widowed, tells me on the phone that she thinks Dad is responsible for the obscene phone calls she received when Mom was out of town on business. She talks about how her daughter had mixed feelings about staying with us: she adored me, but she didn't like Uncle Leland showing her pornography and molesting her. Aunt Margaret says that her daughter complained, and that at one point, Mom walked in on Dad and the little girl. "What did Mom do?" I immediately inquire.

"Just walked back out."

"Why did you let J. (the daughter) stay with us?"

"I always felt like she was safe there."

I cannot believe my ears. I hang up the phone and sit for fifteen minutes staring into space and feeling amazed, astonished, disgusted and incredulous. Now I know for sure that my mother never provided any protection for me. She is an accomplice, and in her own way, a perpetrator. I feel a lot less guilty for having had my friends to lunch to celebrate the anniversary of her death. It's a tradition, now. Everything that's ever happened to me, every thought I've had—all is in question.

My cousin, C, and I are now corresponding regularly. She lives in another state. C is my Aunt Bessie's daughter—the one who lived in Leland's house as a small child. Does she remember anything like this? C is the kind of person who'd have trouble making negative comments about Satan. She has a wonderful sense of humor, a strong Christian faith and willingness to help. Estranged from Craig and me, Dad moved to Arkansas near the end of his life so that C and Aunt Bessie would care for him. Craig and I instantly nominated them both for sainthood. Now some other events come hurtling back into my awareness and taking on new meaning.

From copies of letters C sends me I get a picture of the kind of young man my dad was. I can't figure out how he got this way, but a major contributing factor seems to have been his mother's death in 1931. My grandfather writes to his older son in California describing her death in a letter consisting of one continuous, run-on sentence: "It seams (sic) as if I can't get over it I am so broken in heart and I don't know sometimes what to do I know mama is at rest and is better off than we all are but it seams so hard to hafto give her up I just can't realize that she is gone I can hardly write this letter for the tears blind my eyes. ..." For all his emotion, Grandpa got right on with his life—looking for a third wife. He got somebody in to keep house, and went on, apparently, ignoring his family. Dad's younger sister, who was playing the piano at the church every week, began to get sick. Grandpa, watching her abdomen get bigger and bigger, decided she was pregnant. He seems not to have asked her about this. She didn't have a boyfriend, but that didn't seem to figure into the calculation. C tells me that if my mother's mother had not told him to take Mary Catherine to a doctor, he probably wouldn't have done it. My maternal grandmother, seeing and talking to Mary Catherine almost daily, knew something was really wrong and it wasn't of a moral or spiritual nature. Mary Catherine died in 1932 of ovarian cancer. Dad joined the Navy, and got a trip home from wherever he was just after basic training and before he shipped out. He wrote to his brother (the misspellings are his):

> You ask me about that girl dad has married. I found out that he got the licence about a month ago and that they had left for California.
>
> When I was home on "boot" leave I met her. She was at that time keeping house for dad. Well she fell hard for me, and I could do anything I wanted to? And so I did. Later on I found out that she would go out with anything

that wore pants.

She is from some little hick town in Kentucky about forty miles from Louisville. She married some bootlegger in the hills. They had a child and he didn't treat her right and so she left him. That her story.

They came back from California to soon. They didn't have time to get there and back so I guess there was some trouble on the way and they came back. That is what Elizabeth, my sweetheart, said.

I have forgotten the whole rotten mess. Dad never writes me and I never write him so that is that. ...

We are going to be here untill some time in May. I don't mind a bit because the people here think we are swell. You can snap your finger and have all the women you want. (Boy are my fingers sore?) It is too hard to be true to one girl when she is 1000 miles away and these girls are so good looking?

Once he shipped out on the *Tuscaloosa*, he didn't have a problem with being true to his sweetheart. He didn't bother:

Last Sunday I had the weekend off here in Frisco. Liberty started at 1:30 PM and I made the first boat. We went to a hotel and a couple of rooms. My friend and I went out and drank a bit tried some dancing and what have you. We picked up some women and we did some more drinking and dancing. We bought three qts of liquor and went to the hotel. We stayed up to 4 AM drinking, fighting, loving and what have you? The chippie I had thought she was a singer and a grasshopper all in one. We all were acting up. The next morning (11:45AM) we got up and counted noses and one girl was missing so I let the other fellow have mine. I met a marine officer and he ask me in his room for a few drinks. We drank and talked untill about 4 PM. He got drunk and I wasn't in very good shape my self so I started back to the ship alone. My friend got kicked out of the room and couldn't find me so he left. I got back to the ship O.K. and got some sleep. I felt tough the next day but that was all. Well, that will last me for the next six months a guy has got to let of steam some time. I am just about out of something to write about so I will close.

How is the baby?

I'm aghast as I read these letters because they are just the ones I've seen. I see a pattern now, and it makes me sick to my stomach. I start to wonder how many other people have been affected by him. Maybe others see him as just a typical kid away from home for the first time, testing his limits and sowing his wild oats, but I've heard some of his stories in their relatively sanitized version. I decide to ask C if she remembers any problem. After quite a bit of correspondence, she eventually comes out with the information that not all of her memories of Uncle NeNe (that was her baby name for him) are positive. I realize she doesn't want to remember. A part of

me can't stop trying to track down the genesis of all my mistrust, disgust and depression, but a part of me feels as if I've
opened Pandora's box, and that it's a big mistake. Now I start
to look back at my adult relationship with Dad.

He stopps letting me sit on his lap when I am about
twelve. He says I am too big. I think he has stopped the rap-
ing by then, although I've never known for sure. He continues to tell me dirty jokes, which it annoys him to explain.
When I begin to date not too long after that, he doesn't like
any of my boyfriends. When I go away to college—not a particularly good option from my parents point of view   ("We
just want you to be happy")—I have to get some books to tell
me about sex. I have completely blocked all memories of it
and feel totally naïve. Unsteady on my own and bored with
the classes, I return home at the end of the first semester, and
enroll at the University of Louisville. In a French class, I
meet Herb, whom I will later marry. Herb spends a lot of time
at my house, which pushes a lot of Dad's buttons. He says he
doesn't feel like he can say or do things normally. I guess not.
Somebody from a functional family like Herb would probably
think something was fishy. Dad could keep up his social
façade for a couple of hours at a time, but I didn't know what
a cramp Herb's being there put in Dad's style.

When Mom dies, Dad immediately starts to develop
more obvious and serious problems. His next door neighbor is
a young mother with two little girls. She, at first, tries to be
neighborly. She brings over a meal or two. She knows he is
lonely. She and her daughters become the focus of his interest, and Craig and I don't like it, but we don't interfere. It
isn't very long before the house next door is up for sale.

Dad, a diabetic, has a heart attack. My in-laws call to
inform me of a situation that has gone from bad to worse. He

is sick and near death for months. We clean out the house and put all of his stuff in storage. We call the relatives and decide to move him to Nashville where Craig can look after him. We don't think he is going to live. I ride to Nashville in the ambulance with Dad. It's about a three-hour trip from Louisville, which is now home to Dad only. I am living with my family in Cincinnati where my husband is associate pastor of a large church. Dad makes the trip on the gurney; he has to be helped to the men's room by the ambulance attendants, and we have spotted the hospitals along the route because nobody can be sure he'll make it down there. I am tired. Laura, Jeff and I have been staying with my in-laws for weeks, and their father has come that morning to take them back to Cincinnati. My marriage is beginning to unravel, but I blame it on the fact that I have had to spend so much time taking care of Dad. During the month I spend in Louisville, Herb begins "dating," and, to add insult to injury, takes his new lady friend on bike rides using my bike. He tells me all about it when I get home and is surprised that I do not want to pursue a friendship with the woman.

Despite the critical nature of the trip, Dad survives. Hospitalized for weeks in Nashville, he makes a slow recovery. He goes to live with Craig and his family. As far as I know everything is fine. Craig has to travel for business a lot at this time, so frequently Dad is alone with Rosemary and the two kids. A few months go by. Dad, who has received a fairly large insurance settlement in Mom's death, is dispatched to visit his brother in California and his sister in Florida. This takes a month or so.

One pleasant afternoon, the phone rings. Craig is on the other end. "Meet the plane," he says. "Dad's coming to you because he can't stay here."

The problem, it emerges, is that Dad has been attempting to get Rosemary to sleep with him. When she tells him no way, and that that is inappropriate, he pulls out the gun he has always had with him and threatens to shoot her. She locks herself and the kids up. She should have called the police. When Craig returns from his trip and hears about this, my phone is ringing.

So, Dad stays with me for a while. During the stay, he loses circulation in his legs because he will not stop smoking or take care of his diabetes. Ultimately, he has one leg amputated. Concerned about his being away from the doctors in Nashville who have been treating him, Craig and I decide to bring him back to Nashville and set him up in his own apartment. I have had enough. The strain of being nice to Dad is wearing on all of us. We have a busy life, can't ask babysitters to stay with the kids unless Dad is in the hospital or somewhere, can't leave the kids with him, and I constantly feel uncomfortable around him, both for old and new reasons.

Meanwhile, Aunt Margaret has bought Dad's house in Louisville. She divides it into two living areas and rents part of it. Somehow, Dad wooes and wins her. She sells the place and moves to Nashville. He complains about her and she complains about him to the point where she asks me how upset I'd be if she divorces him. I say, "Not at all." She moves to Florida to be near her daughter, and we think all is well.

I become pregnant, and my marriage is not improving. It is dying a slow death. Herb is into a doctor of ministries program in pastoral counseling. He complains that I don't take enough interest in him, that we need an open marriage, that we should each have our own friends of various genders, although my friends are supposed to be women. Then, Dad has to have the other leg amputated. I sit at the hospital while the surgeons do what they have to do. Able to leave the hospital, finally, Dad is placed in a convalescent home where he incurs the displeasure of all by exposing himself and making lewd remarks to the staff. Craig and I become concerned that Dad's medical expenses will soon outstrip our ability to finance them. Dad likes to play the commodities market where he has no luck at all, and he is a notorious spendthrift. We decides to place the bulk of his money in a trust fund to take care of him, and this is explained and signed at the convalescent facility. Craig's lawyer comes, I fly down and one of the nurses in the facility serves as a witness. Dad seems to think it is a good idea.

Once again, we think we have all the loose ends tied. Dad continues to bother the staff at the home, but, after a while, we are able to get him back in his apartment. At this point, the cult enters upon the scene. A bunch of people mainly interested in tapping into the trust fund (Dad was vocal about having "a lot of money"—not true) begin "love-bombing" him. They take him to four-hour video presentations where he can't leave or ask questions. They convince him that the Bible has it all wrong, and they have it all right. They feed him, spend time with him, take him to the movies, etc. They send a young man to live with him and take care of him. These are the letters I got from Dad during this time— only one has a date on it— so I've put them in the order I think they go in. I have copied them exactly.

Linda

Send the wine decanter—How did you get your hands on it in the first place? Your letters are full of advise which is so wrong its

funny Hell you must have read Dr. Bernes lat-
testbook "I'm sick—your sick". How could you
live so long and still be so dumb? Well it very
simple instead of seeking truth where it is to
be found (The Word) you have chose to listen
to old garbage heart the king of the
Brentwood Castle, that is "Les Palace de
parnoia.

It has taken me three year to see that you
and Craig realy meat what the trust says: that
is to say my well-being has been placed in the
hands of a banker. Didn't you get a copy? Or
has old garbage heart skillfully kept a copy
away from you like he did me. Well three years
is long enough for me and so I will take some
affirmative action to assure my future.

There is a certain church here that will
rewrite my will and help me reassign my insurance and act as exector for my estate. They are
big and have a leagal staff like General
Motors. For this they will take care of all of my
need when I am too feeble to not live alone.
In the mean time I can depend on them for
small services like helping me shop and taking
me any place I want to go. One thing for sure
I won't ever go in a nursing home run for prof-
it I did that bit and its nowhere. I'll close now
as I have a date to-night. Inclosed is a picture
of my girlfriend.

Dad

There is, indeed, a picture of the "girlfriend" mentioned. What we ultimately find out, when Dad sues us for the amount of the trust, is that the "legal" department of the outfit is a real estate lawyer. We easily win, but it is not without cost. I have to testify against him, Aunt Margaret has to fly in and testify against him, as does Craig. We have to bring affidavits and statements from the doctors and staff at the nursing home verifying that he knew what we were doing and agreed to the trust, that he was taking no medications at the time. We have stipulated that he receive all income from the trust and be allowed to pay medical bills from it. Craig has only the right to move the trust to another bank if we don't like the way it is managed. By the time Dad dies, he has made major inroads into the trust having bought several wheelchairs, artificial limbs and so on with an eye to dissipating as much as possible.

Dear Linda-

> Received the pictures of the kids and Karen's paste up It is too bad your greed has cut them of from their grandfather.
>
> Even Presbyterians in thire most enlightened moments must see—that when a person does the devils work, he receives the devils pay. The devil is a poor paymaster, as you are finding out!
>
> I find no place in Gods Word where he (God) condones white collared robbery. Then what else should I expect of people that tell multicolored lies!
>
> The most tricky lie you tell yourself is

called rationatization

How many lies (white of course) have you had to tell your children? How much longer will they believe them? Time is running out for you!

You should add up the debts and credits. You will see your in the red, and this is only starters there is more to come

I could quote you scripture but, I won't, since your trust in is Craig and the Commerce Union Bank in place of God.

Dad

By this time, I no longer let the children open mail from "Grampsie." Since I haven't remembered the sexual abuse yet, I think this is about all of the abuse, but I am wrong. I receive one more letter.

April 27, 1978

Linda

I wish you would quit writing to me and making phone calls. In doing so you add insult to injury. Your communication only serves to remind me of the web of lies and corruption you and your brother used to grab my assets (The desire for money is the root of all evil)

Thank to you and your brother last month I had to kill that banker ass to get money to pay a dental bill and the rent. If this makes you feel badly you can always call your brother and he will rationallize and give you excuses. That viper will vomit forth sweet sounding word and make you feel like you had a shot of coke.

So bugg off

Dad

I quit trying to communicate. By now, I'm suspecting that maybe he's always been a first class asshole. A year goes by. My brother-in-law lives in the same town as my father who sees him once in a while. One day, my phone rings. It is my brother-in-law and he says I must come to Bowling Green, Kentucky because my father is really sick. I phone Dad. He's sick and I tell him I'm coming. It takes half an hour to work myself up to call, five minutes for the call, and an hour and a half of recovery on the living room floor. I am weak in the knees, shaking, sick to my stomach. I am not about to go to Bowling Green alone. My husband will go, and we call Craig and Rosemary. We agree to meet at a small restaurant on the north side of town to plot our strategy. We know that the young man is living in Dad's place—the cult has sent them there to make converts on the Western Kentucky University campus. We have heard, via my brother -in-law, that there is a woman in the picture, although no one seems to know any-thing about her. Aware that Dad always has a gun handy—he kept a loaded shotgun behind our kitchen door all my life, and Rosemary has already had some experience with it—we determine the order in which we'll enter the house. We are only joking a little, out of actual concern. Should we ask the police to meet us there? How many people will be in the house? Will they put up a fight? Nobody knows, but we figure my husband has the least chance of being shot, followed by me, then Rosemary, and, finally, Craig—the most hated of the lot.

Now as I reflect on the history I have with my father, this all comes back with a vengeance. I am still gathering information. C says that our cousin Carolyn has had some similar problems with her father, my dad's brother. This explains some rather strange conversations I have with Carolyn when I visit her in the summer of 1983. I am celebrating having finished some more graduate school. I am now qualified to teach learning disabled or behavior disordered children. I still have a little money left over from my student loan and I have a job for the fall. The children have gone on a cross-country trip to the Sacramento, California area with their father and step-mother. I have been divorced for about a year—this is a kind of wedding tour for him. I make the rounds of relatives on Dad's side. First stop is Fort Smith, Arkansas. Dad lives there now. The cult has also followed him, and he has brought about a thousand Kentucky cockroaches to stay and keep him company as well.

On a trip to Nashville, I stop to see him. This is shortly before his move. The children and I arrive at one of the most miserably rundown duplexes I have ever seen. A crude ramp for the wheelchair bumps down the front porch steps. There is no access to the pitiful backyard for Dad. The house is filthy. Food has been left out, dirty dishes are in the sink and a layer of dust coats everything. The cockroaches are running rampant over the contents of the kitchen cabinets in the middle of the day. They don't even scatter when I'm in there washing every dish before I serve the food I've brought. The children are reluctant to eat anything. The gun is on the desk. My son wants to look at it; the girls are petrified. Dad is trying to be charming to the kids, giving them a bunch of junk he has lying around such as a model steam engine he built, and a world of advice. They want out of there.

After his illness in Bowling Green, his health does not improve, nor does his attitude. He is still mad at Craig, and my relationship with Dad is now rocky. I go to his Arkansas apartment. He is getting Meals on Wheels, but apparently nobody is housekeeping for him. I think my aunt and cousin go a couple of times a week and do what they can, but Dad is a slob. I visit for a few hours, but mainly I visit my cousin and her mother. They put me on a plane to Los Angeles where Carolyn and her family pick me up. During my stay at her house, Carolyn and I have time to talk, and she indicates that the problems I have with my Dad—constant dirty jokes, lewd remarks, exposing himself, etc.—are the same with her father. I learn much later that there was molestation for her, too.

Sadly, only a few months after my visit, Carolyn dies suddenly of a pulmonary embolism, which her doctors say is lucky since the breast cancer she thought she had beaten has, by then, begun to invade her bones. Even after hours of talk with Carolyn, I do not remember. Uncle Jim is still alive, then, but not long after Carolyn's death, Aunt Lucetta (his wife and Carolyn's mother) dies. Uncle Jim then embarks on dating and so on, just like his brother. Jim also has had some adventures, but that's another story. Ultimately, he, too, moves to Arkansas where he later dies. I joke that Arkansas must be our family graveyard, similar to the graveyard where the elephants go to die. Craig and I make a pact that if one of us suddenly has an urge to move to Arkansas, he or she will first contact the sibling.

Dad stays in Fort Smith, but years of neglecting diabetes

have caught up with him He has to go on kidney dialysis. He grows sicker until the doctor calls for Craig and me to come down. Craig and I have grown closer over the last few years. We nearly always have a good time together, even though we have some significantly differing outlooks on our lives. Some subjects we shy away from, but we have similar senses of humor, and like to talk. We are convinced that this is Dad's final round, and are prepared to tell the doctor to pull the plug. Craig's lawyer has drafted a letter explaining our position, which is that if Dad has no likelihood of a comfortable life, then the doctor should make Dad comfortable and let nature take its course. After considerable discussion with the doctor, we give him the letter.

The doctor has wanted me to bring Dad to Cincinnati, but I not only don't want him, I don't think he'll survive the trip. Dad refuses to see Craig at the hospital despite the seven- or eight-hour drive from Nashville that Craig has made on his behalf. When I go into Dad's room, he is exposing himself. I jerk the sheet over him, but I'm too disgusted to touch him at all, so there's no joyous reunion or sad farewell. Dad pretends that he doesn't know what's going on, but I can see him watching me to see my reaction. The man is dying of kidney failure, has suffered cardiac arrest twice in the previous week and, even though the doctors have exercised the do-not-resuscitate orders, Dad has managed to last for one more jab at us.

My cousin C is married to a health professional who advises us not to say anything we don't want Dad to hear. Her husband has attended many dying patients and knows that often, the hearing is the last sense to go. They have been stymied because the hospital wants Dad moved to a nursing home, but no nursing home will take him. That's when the doctor calls me. By the time I get there, it is no longer an issue.

On the way home to Cincinnati, I decide to stop at the funeral home which handled my mother's service and burial ten years earlier. Craig says he doesn't care what I do for a funeral for Dad as long as his major contribution is to show up. I drop in on the way through Louisville, and a slightly paunchy, red-faced, balding man is assigned to my case. I never quite catch his name. He sits me down in a cool, rather dark room with a conference table, arm chairs and a very nice carpet. Uh-oh, I think. I know Dad has insurance, and I sure hope it'll be enough.

"I want to make arrangements for my father's funeral," I say.

"Oh," he says sadly. "When did he pass away?"

"Well, he didn't—yet. He's about to die in Fort Smith, Arkansas, but he has a slot in the Evergreen Mausoleum, and we'll have to bring him up here."

"How did you select our home?"

"You did my mother's service."

"When was that?"

I give him the pertinent information and he's off. He hauls out a huge registry book, thumbs the index and turns to a page. There, in beautiful cursive, is all anyone could ever want to know about the details of burying my Mom.

"What do I have to do? I don't have a lot of time," I tell him.

"If something should happen to your father. ..."

"Something's *going* to happen to my father. I just don't know when exactly, but it won't be long—maybe a week at most. I'm just driving through and I want to get all this arranged so I don't have to do it long distance next week or whenever." My complete calm but slight irritation is getting to him. He is making a big assumption—that I care a whole lot about this. I don't. I'm doing what has to be done. If it were okay, legal and I could stand the smell, I'd have no problem dumping the old goat back behind my garbage cans, but such is not the case. And I haven't even remembered the abuse yet.

"Well, you'll have to pick out a casket. Your mother has this beautiful cherry wood model."

I know that costs more than I want to spend, so I ask, "What difference does that make?"

"You want them to match, don't you?"

"No. These boxes are never going to be seen together."

"People will remember."

"I doubt it. My brother and I will be about the only ones there who were at Mom's funeral."

"How did your mother die?"

"Accident. Decapitated in a car wreck. What casket choices do I have?" His shock and my nonchalance almost ruin his spiel.

He takes me to the macabre showroom where a couple dozen casket styles are propped open revealing the drapery inside. There are all sizes and colors. Some are metal, some are wood. He leads me over to a casket similar to my mother's. I repeat that I don't think matching the caskets is important. He extols the virtues of metal—they're more expensive, they'll last longer. I'm never sure whether I was able to bite my tongue or whether "So what?" actually came out of my mouth.

"How about this one?" I ask, indicating a rather short, blue model.

"Oh, no, no, no," he says. "It's too short. It's for a woman."

"My Dad's short now—he's a double amputee. He'd fit."

Gasps. I think this man may require medical assistance. I have, up to now, seen no reason to bring this amputation business up. "I still can't sell you that one. What does your brother prefer?"

"He doesn't care. I can do whatever I want."

"Oh, dear." He is clearly wondering what family of ogres spawned me. I ask a few more prices and settle on an oak model that looks pretty good. It is medium priced, no one will be embarrassed by it and it's not going in the ground, so how long it lasts is immaterial. "What color do you want inside? This one comes in beige or blue. You can have (here he tells me about some kind of insert or padding for under the body)."

"Okay. Beige. And just the box as is."

The session is far from over, I learn to my dismay. Now we have to go into body preparation.

"Now, what is your father going to wear?"

"What does he need?"

"Underwear, suit, shirt, socks, shoes ... oh, goodness! I said it! I'm sorry!"

"What did you say?"

"I said, 'shoes.'" The anguished look on his face almost makes me giggle.

"That's okay. We joke about it all the time—tell him we're giving him socks for Christmas. Don't worry. I'm not offended."

"He'll need a full set of clothing. Does he have a suit?"

"I guess so. The funeral home in Arkansas will put something on him. My aunt or cousin will get clothes from his apartment."

"Well, then. Do you want our cosmeticians to make him up?"

"No. We aren't opening this box. You get him in it and

close it."

"What side does your father part his hair on? This side, like mine, or the other side."

"I don't know, but it doesn't matter. We aren't opening the casket."

"You'll want to greet family and friends. Shall I book you for the evening before the service?"

"No. Everybody is coming from out of town. Just put him wherever you want until the graveside service."

"What if someone wants to see him?"

"Let them. But I just saw him yesterday. He looks terrible, and I don't think he'll look any better when he gets here. Nobody wants to see him. If somebody asks you to open the box, it's their problem. But I don't think that'll happen. This is going to be short, and a very small group. Can you take him to Evergreen?" Evergreen Cemetery is about a mile and a half down the street from where we're sitting."

"Yes. That's part of our service. Now what about pallbearers?"

"What do I need pallbearers for? You just drop him off in the chapel at Evergreen, right? Then the cemetery people take it from there. I called them already."

"Our people can only move the casket ten feet. If it has to go further than that, you need pallbearers. We have some nice gentlemen who can do that for you for a small charge."

"How far is it from the hearse to the chapel? Don't you have some kind of gurney or trolley for the casket? If it has to be moved by us, I don't see a real problem. My brother, my nephew, my son and my uncle will be there, and I'm pretty sure we can get a couple of other guys if we need to."

"Well, these gentlemen ..."

"That's okay. We'll handle it." These are probably the

same guys who go on cruises to see that all the ladies have a good time, I think.

He's giving up, now. He's finally understanding that we are not a family who feel compelled to give our "loved one" the entire luxury send-off. "What about limousines?"

"Limousines? No. We'll just all get to the cemetery in our own cars. There won't be many, and besides, no one will need to come here."

"Are you sure you don't want to use one of our viewing rooms?"

"I'm sure. Now do I just call you and let you know when he's coming?"

"Yes. What about flowers?"

"Oh, yeah. My ex-father-in-law was a florist. I'll just call the new owner of the store, and they'll send out something."

I'm exhausted and hungry. It's suppertime and I still have two hours to drive. I am, furthermore, expected at my ex-in-laws for dinner (I only divorced one member of that family). I am trying to wind this whole thing up. I've had to take time off from my recently acquired job to deal with all this, my divorce still hurts and my children are stressed out trying to field a new stepmother, two sick grandfathers (their Dad's father has Parkinson's Disease and is bedfast), school and the advice of one and all. "Is that everything?"

I eventually get out of there. When Dad dies about four or five days later, all I have to do is call the funeral home. I believe that the body driven up from Arkansas to Louisville is Dad's, and I believe that every legal t is crossed and every i dotted. The box stays closed. It sits in a back storage room at the funeral home ready to go on the appointed day. I meet my uncle at the airport.

It's a dry-eyed group that gathers at Evergreen Chapel

that morning. We don't need pallbearers, but my uncles, nephew and son are asked to walk the casket up to the front. People are milling around, chatting, reading the names on the niches in the mausoleum. It is very modern and cool. The funeral home people leave and we're on our own. Members of the cult have come to stare daggers at us and accuse us of not loving our father. This last point is well-taken, but I don't care. I am filled with relief that I do not have to put up with him any more. Today is the last time I have to deal with him.

That turns out to be a little fairy tale I've concocted for myself. My dad, I later discover, is far from dead. Sure, his body is gone, but, to paraphrase an old song, the malady lingers on. I haven't got any inkling of what I'm in for once the immediate problem is solved. I know already that Dad is an abuser and a pervert, but I really haven't grasped the extent to which it affects me. All I know is that I feel mostly embarrassed that all these people are obligated to come to Louisville to see him off, as it were, and not one of them cares any more than I do. I feel guilty that I don't care, that I'm relieved, and think my life is going to be better now. Twenty years later, I'll stop feeling bad about not feeling bad.

There's not much talk about the deceased. I have called a professor from Louisville Presbyterian Theological Seminary, who is also a family friend, to do the service. Here, again, Craig has given me carte blanche. I have told my friend very little about Dad, so the service is generic and mercifully short. The only uncomfortable part is that the cult has sent two or three representatives who apparently have come to glower at us and shake their heads disapprovingly. These men are middle-aged, and so somber, stern and dark-looking that they invite ostracism. The relatives and friends attempt to greet them, but they are focused on trying to make everyone else feel their pain, so they are somewhat successful, even though we quickly move to ignoring them. They don't come to the lunch afterwards that Craig has set up in a meeting room at the motel where we are all staying. The folks who do come have a fine afternoon visiting with each other, and by about three o'clock they have mostly headed back to wherever they traveled from. We take Dad's brother to the airport, then start back home ourselves.

In 1991, I have to reflect on all this. I have to determine how I coped, and what else there is to know. Age forty-eight is a hell of an age to have to remember what has colored my life in dark shades, alienated two husbands, made me question every action I've ever taken, worry that my children may have been abused and, most of all, wonder what I could have been and done. I slowly acquire some answers, but it makes me angry.

Sing a Song of Little Girls

Sing a song of little girls,
Flat-chested, lean, sun-browned little girls,
In the green, green yard standing in the dappled shade,
Wearing clean white panties.

Sing a song of little girls,
Long hair, tossed by breezes, tangled, in ribbons,
Eyes wide with emotion, wet with tears.
Don't be scared, it's only a game.

Sing a song of little girls,
No more than eight years old and thinking
All the daddies do this, don't they?
Now, don't tell. This is our secret.

Sing a song of little girls,
Innocence gone, but ignorant still,
The sour, acrid tastes and smells never leave them,
Though they "forget" what happened.

Sing a song of little girls,
Not little anymore, and not grown either,
Warped and shaped by evil, all trust shattered,
Betrayed by a lover.

Five

I'm going to get the baby mole!" Daddy is digging his fingers into my groin area where a small, brown freckle is located. I am screaming in some pain, but mostly frustration, and gasping for a breath that is so hard to catch. He's holding me down, and he's relentless. I can't get away. This happens every day. He plays with me constantly. The assumption is that I'm screeching with laughter because I like it so much.

Years later, recalling this scene, it occurs to me that I really do get away from him the only way I can figure out how to do. I slip out of my body mentally and become another person. This person can be seen in pictures of me taken when I was small. She has a rather vacant look because the real me is a million miles inside, hiding out in her. I give her a name, Nancy. I don't know why it is, but whenever someone has trouble thinking of my name, they'll call me Nancy every time. I ask Louisville David, Therapist David and another friend, Wayne, about this, but they don't have any explanation.

Nancy is the person I've grown up with. She is not like my imaginary friend, Mary Lou. Nancy has a bigger role to play in my life. As a very little girl, I thought of Nancy as a doll I crawled inside. She took the abuse because she could ignore the feelings. Nancy has always functioned in a very mature manner. She meets and greets other people; she does well in school. Nothing bothers her. Looking at pictures of me, one sees Nancy in the faraway gaze and the artificial smile. Nancy does what she's told to do. She is an ideal little girl with a very tough hide. She only thinks about how to save me from the ugliness of being raped most days and how to keep it out of my mind. My self fades away.

Now that I know Nancy, I start to meet the others. They are Linnie, a child of about two or three, the girl in the tank—no name—about age seven or eight, and Ted, a teenager about sixteen or seventeen, rebellious, smart-mouthed and the only male persona. Nancy's main job is to keep the others out of sight and hearing of Mom and Dad. A teacher once told me, "You have the blackest moods of any-body I ever saw!" She saw Nancy hard at work protecting the others and me. When I meet Nancy as a separate part of myself, I am nearly overwhelmed by the terror of seeing my real self in contrast. Placid, stoic Nancy is covering up a cow-ering, screaming, petrified little girl in a "mommy costume," a phrase innovated by my son one time, only he said I was "a strong man" in a "mommy costume." Costume or no, I am no "strong man." I still can't talk much about the terror, but I think I can write about it now. Holocaust, prisoner torture such as we've learned about recently in Iraq, serial killers and sex crimes stir me as I identify with the victims. I feel much of their pain and humiliation, their loss of control and their helplessness. The stab in the belly, the ice-cold hand on the back of the neck, the churning in the stomach and the will-ingness to do anything to get away from there—these feelings are familiar to me. My mother is the terrorist. In the name of raising a beautiful and accomplished daughter, she has reduced me to a quivering, quavering, jelly of a coward hiding out in a complex mental defense system that is pretty nearly impregnable by the time I'm eight.

The girl in the tank points this out to me. She is in an old military tank. The tank has tracks, but doesn't move. I don't know if the guns work, but they are there, and they make her feel safer. Nobody can get near this tank. It's parked in a meadow, green, flowery, and there's always comfortable weather. The girl looks out of the tank to watch out for Mom and Dad, but under no circumstances does she leave the tank. She is able to leave, but she chooses not to. She doesn't actually know Nancy and is unaware of Linnie, who is nearby behind a big rock. She doesn't know Ted either, but she doesn't want company anyway. The trouble is that until she got into the tank, nearly every encounter with another person was traumatizing. She lost consciousness of everything except staying alone and safe. Without realizing it, she lets Nancy carry the ball.

Mom tells Nancy how to act and what to say. Nancy learns very nice manners because Mom serves a Sunday dinner every week, complete with her best dishes on a tablecloth at the dining room table. Mom cooks artichokes so Craig and Nancy can learn how to eat exotic things when they're out at some fancy party or dinner. Mom believes that her children will rise to great heights in the world and may need to know how to address royalty or eat dinner with the President. Before Nancy is fully developed as an alter personality, I receive a small part in a Sunday School play. I am the first one on the program. Mom drills me for weeks to say: "A long, long speech I will not make. A lot of time it will not take.

The speech, like me, is very small. It's welcome and Merry Christmas to you all." I've got it nailed, complete with gestures and inflection. On the night of the big performance, my mother is embarrassed thoroughly, but laughs it off for years and years-literally. Nancy does not recollect this incident at all, but I am told that before I made my speech, I hiked my new dress up and showed the crowd my panties. "See?" I am reported to have said. "They're new!" In the household I grew up in, that is just the sort of thing that happened all the time. One's underwear or private parts could be inspected at any time and judgment would be passed on the quality of the merchandise, one might say. To me, it is simply natural to want to share the happy news that I have new lace-trimmed underwear with my church family. Everybody laughs. I am confused because Mom hasn't covered this particular subject in her "making a public appearance" unit. Nancy picks up on the laughter and immediately stores my embarrassment in some kind of hermetically sealed Miracle Whip jar of the mind. I don't see it again for almost fifty years.

Nancy is so there for me, that I forget who I really am. Nancy senses the vibes from adults. She screens them and decides what to do from there. One day when I am less than school-age, my Uncle Robert comes by to see my mother. I am in the backyard playing with my dolls and Mom is in the basement doing the laundry in an old electric wringer wash-er. The weather is warm and sunny. I am glad to be out of the basement and away from Mom since she usually has some Linda improvement project going on. I want no part of that!

A strange man enters the yard and asks if my mother is home. "Wait out here," I say. "I'll get her." He chuckles, but he waits. I run through the open cellar door—two slanted halves—and down the concrete steps and through a second, conventional door into the basement. "Mama. There's a strange man outside. He wants to see you." "Stay here," she says. She turns off the washer in case I decide to put my hand in the wringer while she's gone. She regularly thinks I'm just about to do something truly stupid at any moment. She goes outside and I stand in the basement holding my ever-present doll. In seconds, she's back with the man and they are laughing. "This is your Uncle Robert," she informs me. "He's my brother." "She sure knows her Ps and Qs," he remarks.

I do not know Uncle Robert because I've never seen him before. He's the preacher brother and he lives somewhere out of town (turns out to be Lockland, Ohio, on Cincinnati's northern side). How would I know he's somewhat estranged from the family? They rarely mention him except in whispers. I don't know whether he's bad, good or what. I just know that Nancy will keep me from as much danger as possible.

I don't call her Nancy in my head. She seems such a part of me that I mix us up, and after a few years, it's just Nancy. There's no Linda. Nancy has met Jesus in person on a few occasions. Once, he comes and sits by her bed at night. He doesn't do anything, but she can kind of see him, just there. She feels his benevolent spirit, although he doesn't say anything either. Another time, she slips up and speaks out loud to Jesus in Mom's presence. It takes a lot of side-stepping and agreeing that she can't control her mouth to get out of that one. Nancy never shares any real feeling of any kind with Mom, and she can't admit that Jesus has walked into the room for just a second. Mom has enough to work on.

Mom tells Nancy how to feel, and this is rather convenient in a peculiar way. Mom defines social situations for the young Nancy in this manner. If I scrapes my knee, I get merthiolate on it, an admonition to watch where I am going and the information that the stinging will stop soon; it doesn't. She lectures and argues if I don't stop crying and pretend to feel fine. If I feel sad, I'm not sad. I'm tired, getting sick, being silly or should forget it. There is always a distraction for a feeling Mom doesn't want to deal with. She attempts to use humor and distraction to steer me away from reality. When I have measles, I am stuck in a darkened room for about two weeks covered with the typical rash. Mom decides I might be amused to look at the rash, although I have indicated no interest in finding out how I look with the measles. She brings a mirror in the room and professes surprise when I start to cry and say, "I'll never be pretty again!" This story is hilarious when repeated to the neighbors and relatives.

Mom needs me to be good and not cause any trouble because Craig is having a lot of his own struggles and she has to spend a lot of time trying to help him out. Nancy takes an almost evil delight in being the "good child," especially in Dad's eyes. Nancy will eat just about anything and say she likes it since Craig is picky. Dad, who loves shrimp, avocado and other foods not locally produced, thinks it's wonderful for Nancy to eat this stuff because it gives him an opportunity to berate Craig for liking only meat and potatoes. Nancy is Daddy's girl. She's sees herself as more important to him than Mom. Mom spends much of the time protecting Craig from Dad and using Nancy as the distracter. Nancy just ignores what they say about her, leaves the room whenever the subject of Linda comes up, plays by herself and reads.

Nancy perceives her job as a defense against the rest of the world. No one is going to get close enough to Linda to hurt her. Nobody is going to know what Linda really thinks or feels because Nancy has them all psyched out, knows what will impress whom, and when to make Linda disappear and block out things. It is likely Nancy who finds the tank, finally, and puts the little girl inside it. Now she doesn't have to worry about Linda so much.

Teachers find Nancy a refreshing change from her more argumentative brother. Nancy gets along with adults, and she is sneaky. She gets the job of cleaning up the first aid room at school. This room overlooks her classroom so she can see what's going on in there. Nancy finds music and math boring. Music is boring because she's taken music lessons for four years. She can read it, sing and play the piano. Do-re-me and 1, 2, 3 are useless to somebody who doesn't have to learn by rote. Nancy reads the A, B, C, D, E, F, G staff, can tell what the time signature is, the key, the names of all the lines and spaces. She rides her bike to her piano lesson every week. Math doesn't interest her because it's a little bit hard, and she can't stand the teacher's dry explanations which don't tell her much anyway. Dad is good at math and gets a kick out of helping Nancy with math homework. So, Nancy knows when it's math or music time and that's the time she cleans the first aid room. She makes the job last as long as necessary by checking out the window to see what's going on in the classroom. There is no supervision for this job.

Nancy has learned from earlier school experience not to be cocky. As a second grader, she rides the last bus every day (still does) and she doesn't like her teacher at all. She figures she's old enough to make it out to the front steps of the school on her own. She tells Mrs. W. that she needs a drink of water. The class is held in a "portable," a temporary structure outside the main building. When Mrs. W. says, "Okay," Nancy goes, gets a drink, but doesn't come back. Mrs. W. follows her, brings her back to the classroom, and invites her to the "round table tea " which is held after lunch every day. This is not an invitation to be desired. Mrs. W. puts all her recalcitrant students around a table in the classroom, heads in the center, bottoms sticking out. She goes around the table swatting each child. Some cry, but not Nancy. Nancy smart-mouths Mrs. W.: "When I tell my daddy about this, he'll bring his gun over here and shoot you." This is more of a possibility than Mrs. W. realizes, though Dad never actually intervenes in any conflict or punishes Nancy in any way. That's Mom's job.

Mom takes it seriously, too. She keeps a switch on top of the refrigerator and brags to her friends and family that she only has to reach for the switch to get me to follow orders. I recall being chased up the stairs to my room by Mom wielding a belt. It's not unusual. It's embarrassing, but true. My mother tells everybody everything about me. There are no secrets, no confidentiality. She tells my aunts whenever she's given me Fletcher's Castoria, which is frequently. Her obsession with my bowels is enormous. She tells what I've said or done, whether it's good or bad. Nancy keeps me from responding to this. She pretends not to hear Mom on the phone with Aunt Margaret or Aunt Bertie. Nancy suggests that we play in our room or outside. In summer, we roam the rows of tomatoes, eating a few along the way. In winter, we put on a sweater to play dolls in the unheated upstairs room that's ours. Nancy is like an identical twin who can stand in for me. I have two emotional outlets by the time I'm eight: I am writing stories and poems (regrettably I don't save but one) and I play the piano. My writing is considered play, and I am not encouraged to keep it around unless it's something for school. School achievement is highly prized. I see Craig as my main competition because Mom boasts about his achievement more than mine.

Because she's active in the PTA, Mom is privy to a lot of information the other mothers can't get. Once, every kid in school takes an IQ test. Educators believed (and still do, to some extent) that knowing one's IQ score has a negative impact on school performance—namely, kids with low scores will quit on the grounds that they are too stupid to learn, and kids with high scores will quit because they will think they are too smart to have to work. Mom pokes in the records and finds our IQ scores. They are high, so she braggs to the relatives and tells Craig and me that we'd better live up to those scores. Today, we know that IQ scores are merely an indicator of verbal and math skills. They don't measure talents in areas besides academic, they don't tell how a person will use the skills he or she has and they certainly don't limit a person's achievement. Back then, Mom believes she has a pair of geniuses on her hands and she devotes herself to our elementary and high school educations.

When Craig wins a scholarship that allows him to skip his senior year and go straight on to the University of Louisville, Mom is thrilled. The fact that Craig is not ready emotionally or socially for college at that time does not figure into the mix. He would have managed much better had his youth been taken into account. I, on the other hand, am under no obligation to go to college. Mom wants me settled with a family, although she sees the wisdom of having "something to fall back on" should my husband die. Hers didn't die, so maybe it is wishful thinking. Nancy and I decide then and there that we are going to college. Our dream to run away from home now has shape and form. Mom and Dad are not prepared to finance this dream, but they tell us they'll figure out something.

Holding My Heart

I hold my heart in my hand,
An alien entity: valves, chambers,
Tubes like hoses bent, of tender flesh.

I've heard the heart can be worn, unprotected, on a sleeve.
Mine won't fit. It's three-dimensional,
Pulsates, quivers, needs me to hold it in my left hand,
Cover it with my right.

I've never seen my heart before.
It hurts to look inside it,
But I don't cry.

So hurt, like one in a coma,
I don't feel my heart in my hand,
But only see it.

— *Six* —

ancy is me. Nancy is the person people know and interact with. I think I am Nancy and I don't have a sense of myself at all. I have no feelings, at least, none that last for more than a few seconds. I am sick for a few moments when Daddy starts kissing me with his open mouth. I truly want to throw up and would if Nancy's plastic face didn't kick in. I only think about it, though, at the very beginning, and when Dad teases me by folding his lips out as far as they'll go so that as much of the inside as possible is showing. He says, "Here's a kiss for you!" Then he flips them out and comes for me. I zone out, as it were. As an adult I believe that's why I like medications that knock me out so much, and I understand how people can become addicted to them. But I have Nancy from way back when, so I don't need drugs.

The sexual behavior and the teasing are relentless. If I'm instructed to bend over to pick something up, Dad swats my behind and says, "Exposed! Exposed!" If there's an odor in the bathroom, it's a cause for comment and study. Aerosol air freshener is not yet on the market. We keep the window open a little. If I pass gas, everybody laughs and mother tells me

91

that it's not nice, that I should go to the bathroom. So when I follow those directions, unfortunately in the midst of an impromptu piano recital demanded by mother for the entertainment of guests, this story makes all the rounds of the family and friends. It's hilarious. Now I'm afraid of any kind of body function, so I begin to try to control them all. I use the bathroom when the coast is clear—Mom is busy somewhere, Dad is outside or in the basement and my brother is holed up in his room.

I do not report illness because every detail will be broadcast to friends and relatives. The neighbors reminisce about the time I had to have an enema because some of them were invited. This retelling occurs at a cook-out my parents are hosting to thank the neighbors for helping with some household project. My screaming and fighting, apparently, were phenomenal. All I remember is the absolute terror of being helpless, held down, humiliated, knowing no reason for this treatment and physical discomfort. During "stories," I go inside the house for about half an hour, not so long that Mom will be worried that I am having trouble in the bathroom (her usual thought), but long enough for the topic to change. I am used to embarrassment by now.

My response, however natural, provides much grist for the family teasing mill. Another time when I am ill, Dad threatens to take my temperature rectally, then yells to Mom in the kitchen, "I'll hold her down, you give her the enema." Mom doesn't hesitate to threaten me this way either. Later, she even suggests an enema for my own child to "scare her a little." This is ridiculous, of course, because my child has no clue as to what that is in the first place, and completely trusts me to do whatever is needed to make her comfortable. By age six, I no longer say the words that refer to elimination or ways to bring it about. I still do not say those words.

I am no fan of staying home with illness since that is a recipe for misery. My mother is a freak about milk toast, too, She's constantly offering to make it for me when I'm sick, regardless of the illness. No food makes me so nauseous, but if I let on that I don't like it, Dad is sure to spend considerable time asking if I don't want some. I want to be left alone. My entire fantasy life consists of ways I can get out of the house. I ask if a person could live on vegetable soup alone. There is discussion. I wish I could lock myself in the bathroom where I'd have the sewer system and water, and live on vegetable soup. I have no ambition other than to live by myself.

I have learned to share nothing. Nancy protects me, and most of the time, I can outfox Mom. She makes me wear undershirts to school. I wear them, take them off in the girls' restroom as soon as I get there and put them back on just before the final bell rings. She has me wear leggings under my dresses to school, the heavy wool kind that go with my winter coat. They're in the coat room in less than five minutes, and don't come out until time to go home. She buys me a new coat, makes a show of giving me a choice about it. I choose a blue coat, but I get the red one. The telling argument, from Mom's point of view, is that my Aunt Elinor would like the red one better. The idea is that I want to be just like Aunt Elinor, and would agree with any of her opinions. I do love my Aunt Elinor and value her opinion, but I know to let Mom dress her dollbaby any way she wants to. I never want anything, I do not have an opinion, I do not make choices. I do exactly as I'm told and look for my chance to escape. It comes in the form of a college education, however, it doesn't immediately work out the way I want it to.

Meanwhile, I'm Barbie's stand-in. I have clothes of every

type except for costumes. Mom is only into serious fashion, although she agrees to make a couple of angel costumes for a church pageant. When I graduate from high school, I have several new outfits: a lavender print dress with a solid lavender jacket; a mint green dress I'd have to see a picture to remember; a dress for the graduation itself despite the fact that the students wear caps and gowns. I nearly faint from the heat and menstrual cramps at the baccalaureate service. I spend all day in bed while my aunts attempt to cure me, including the suggestion that I sit in a hot tub with a cut onion. Mom nixes that one as she says my "womb is open" and I could get an infection. My cramps are the entertainment of the day for the ladies. The men smoke in the backyard.

At my insistence, and due to the fact that my teachers promote it as I am a member of the National Honor Society, I am allowed to try out college. This is an occasion for intense sewing on Mom's part. Suddenly, I do not have a wardrobe. I will need wool skirts, dresses, blouses, sweaters, socks, underwear—everything. Mother is afraid I won't do laundry or find the dry cleaners or will have some occasion come up for which she is unprepared. Mom is working in the department store and she shops every lunch hour for more stuff for me. Evenings and weekends, I do a lot of housework so she can sew for me. Up to now, I have just had to do the cooking. The neighbor kids who have replaced me with Dad ask him, "Who is she? Is she your cooker?" when I come out to the back porch to ask him something. Nancy and I can't wait to pack up the car and take off. My parents know next to nothing about campus life, so whatever I tell them, as long as Craig doesn't get wind of it, goes. He knows what goes on. The only advice I get from anybody is from Craig: "Don't join any Communist cell organizations." No problem.

Murray State College is my favorite teacher's alma mater. It is a beautiful old campus in the southwest corner of Kentucky, near Paducah. Now it's a university. It takes five hours of driving to get there from Louisville because there is no highway the whole way. The route takes us through the "Pennyrile" region of Kentucky—hills and valleys, farm after farm, nothing but pig paths and tiny towns. The famous blue-grass covers the hills, cows stare out at passing cars, there are no rest areas. My clothes are laid out in banana boxes and I have a small, four-drawer chest for my sweaters. Recalling years of escape to a week of summer church camp each year has me pumped for the experience.

Nancy can only stay away at college for one semester. I have worked for my Uncle Ralph as an assistant to Aunt Margaret in running their business. Uncle Ralph is a master plumber, employing most of his nieces and nephews some-where along the line. I also babysit. I save all the money I need for the first semester and refuse all scholarships because I don't want to have to make good grades for anybody but myself. Then I discover that the chemistry class is using the same textbook I'd used in high school, and the English pro-fessor tells me I might find her class boring because I've read all the authors on her syllabus and know my way around a library. So I decide to go home to the University of Louisville when the term is over. There's more challenge there.

Nancy likes being away and so do I, but I am ill-prepared to deal with campus life. Most of the people there are normal. I think I'm normal, too, but I find that I am very different from all of them. I am a small fish in a big pond. It turns out that one needs to be a music major to sing in the chorus because there are enough music majors to be a very fine cho-rus; no "undecided" or history majors need apply. The school newspaper will publish a poem I write, but I can't be on the staff because I'm not a journalism major. I'm majoring in English because my favorite teachers are all English majors. I still send poetry to one of my high school teachers for critique because there is not another person I've encountered who has any clue about creative writing. I am not fitting into campus life very well. Nobody provides me with any direction what-soever. Freshman orientation consists of two plenary sessions of about an hour and a half each. I have no academic advisor because freshmen have so many required courses that there's really no need. No adult attempts to give me any informa-tion.

I've left my boyfriend of three years to come to college. He is staying in Louisville, but when I get back we don't get together at all. I don't think he has another girlfriend, but we're both over it. I've dated at Murray, but only about three guys. I'm awkward on dates. Nancy is entirely too suspicious of everybody's motives. There's no such thing as a simple friendship with a boy. I don't enjoy my dates. My high school sweetheart is a kind of nerdy, immature kid, and although we do some necking, we mostly talk, go to parties at somebody's house, see movies and drink a lot of root beer. The college "men" are basic misfits as well. They aren't bad-looking, but they are pretty inept socially, like me. I know how to eat arti-chokes and be polite to my elders, but I have no idea how to be a friend to my peers. Apparently, I'm likeable, but I form no close relationships with anybody. I eat meals with my roommates—both of them are kind of nerdy, too—or by myself. Greek societies are not extremely strong on this cam-pus. I guess there are some, but I cannot pledge anyway being a freshman. Drinking is not a big pasttime in the circles I run in, and besides, Calloway County is dry.

For a big day, I go down to the town square in Murray. It really is square. On Saturdays, the benches around the courthouse are filled with older men, many in overalls and straw hats, talking. A few Mom and Pop stores are around the square—cleaners, dry goods, grocery and so on. I get a supply of chewing gum, maybe a few crackers to keep in my room. I walk around, sometimes with someone else, but usually alone. The bookstore is close to campus, so I don't go there on these Saturdays. When I've had enough excitement, I stand on the "hitching corner" and get a ride back to campus. Somebody is always willing to drive a bunch of kids back to the school.

Football games are the main weekend activity in Murray. To my surprise, people dress up for the games. I put on my Sunday clothes, heels and the whole outfit to walk the quarter mile or so from my dorm to the football field. I only go if I have a date. Women are not allowed to wear pants or shorts in the lobby of the dorm unless they are passing through on the way to a picnic or participation sport. Freshmen women have to be in the dorm for the night at nine o'clock on week nights and eleven o'clock on weekends unless special permission has been granted. After the football games, we go to the student union for soft drinks and hamburgers. There's no movie theater in Murray. Once in a while, some group, usually a campus group, puts on a show. Headliners are not often seen in Murray.

One of the reasons I go to church is that I can sing in the choir, and it's something to do. There's an attempt to get a college-age youth group going, but I only make it a few times. This would involve more interaction with other people than Nancy is prepared for. Partly to annoy my parents, I date a Jewish boy and a Polish boy from St. Louis. When one of those boys asks, "What are your bad days?" I wonder at the nerve of asking me about when my periods are until he makes it clear that he wants to know what days are heavily scheduled with classes. I am a basic doofus.

When I get back to Louisville, I live at home. Dad does not have a lot of time for me. No longer little and cute, out of his league intellectually, I am more of an aggravation than anything. He is glad, though, that I am back to do the cooking. Mom is working full time. I go to school, come home, study and go to bed. I do not drive because I wrecked a car when I was sixteen, and have been afraid since then. Dad, teaching me to drive, is impatient. He indicates to me that I'm not so good at driving. One Sunday, as I am driving home from church—Dad and Mom have stopped going and he has come to pick me up—I overshoot our drive. "Turn! Turn!" Dad yells at me. So I turn right into the sweet gum tree at the end of our drive. The car is totaled, I am bruised and sore and Dad is sore in a completely different way. Thus endeth my driving. My uncle sends me a poem parody on Joyce Kilmer's "Trees." He writes, "... poems are made by fools like me, but only Linda can maim a tree." Even I think it is kind of funny, but I am embarrassed. This uncle lives in Florida, so my mother is still spreading my fame or shame to the United States. I go to school on the bus when I enroll at U of L.

My brother suggests that the way to buck the lines of people enrolling is to go to the student union and buy a cup of coffee. I should take the steaming cup (and all my paperwork) up to the front door and say the coffee is for Dr. Ekstrom or Dr. Rovett or somebody. The idea is that the door guard will let me in. I then can take the coffee to one of those persons and proceed to enroll in whatever classes I want. I actually never try it, but it sounds like it would work.

Instead, I spend hours with the catalog choosing courses and default courses in case some of them are full when I get in. My parents are now footing the bill. My grades from Murray are good—I get credit for nearly all of the classes I took there—so my folks think I might make it at U of L, but nobody's holding his or her breath. In my gym class—folk dancing—there is one African-American young man. I report this at home with a certain amount of glee. I am not disappointed.

"Who in the world dances with him?" Mom asks. "Do you dance with him?"

"Of course I dance with him. We all do. He's a very nice boy."

One day, the dean of women sends for me. I get a letter from her in the mail and have no idea what she wants. Nancy goes to her office for me because Linnie is too afraid. The dean tells me that one of the sororities on campus is in a decline and can't seem to scare up sufficient pledges of adequate merit to build up the group. She has asked several young women, including me, to pledge this sorority. She cites my many activities in high school, such as four years of choir (I lettered), editing the school newspaper (it won awards), Beta Club, National Honor Society and so on. This sorority needs a shot in the arm. Nancy realizes that we'd never make it through rush in any of the other sororities. We've been around to some and the only one that might have us is a local group with which we are not impressed. So we agree to pledge the struggling sorority, even though Linnie is worried about hazing and initiation. Nancy convinces her that this is an easy way to make friends and get involved socially. All our high school friends are out of our life by now for one reason or another.

We are in trouble from the beginning. The sisters are, naturally, a little offended that they've come to this pass. The pledges get it easy because the sisters don't dare blackball any of us. When the alters get cathected like this, Nancy has all she can do to keep the exterior looking normal. Linda is generally numb or floating around somewhere inside.

Pledging is nothing much, considering how we pledges have been selected. Once a week, we clean up the house and cook dinner for the actives. We have a pledge meeting once a week to learn all of Zeta Tau Alpha's secrets. Nancy and I suggest that since nobody lives in the sorority house but we all live at home with parents, we get our fathers to help with the maintenance of the place. Maturity has, thus far, escaped us. Normal kids in their late teens know how ludicrous a notion this is. The idea is to get away from parents, not invite them into whatever the kids might be doing. Nancy and I consider it a source of free labor. We don't want to hang out with our Dad, either, but we don't know why. The sorority house is wonderful for staying away from home, but nobody lives in any of the Greek houses. We have dinner and a meeting at the house once a week, and we all have keys so that we can use the house between classes or to gather in the evenings. I go there only between classes or to mandatory meetings. If I have to stay on campus during the early afternoon, I bring a sack lunch or go to the Cardinal, which is a student hangout (as far as I know, it still is) serving not-bad hamburgers and the usual trimmings. Once a month, I go to the Presbyterian youth effort on campus, but it's small and struggling, and I don't make friends. I know about three Presbyterians at this time in my life, so I don't have a church connection to anybody in the group.

No sooner are we initiated and made actives, then the

sisters plan rush parties to get new girls in. They do give out pledge class awards. I am the best pledge scholar—I've got the best grade average of all of them. I am now assigned to take girls out on "Coke dates" and to be in attendance at a number of parties so I can chat up and size up other girls. Nancy and I don't do social well. We are usually hiding out somewhere, and, besides, we now have another interest.

Herb is in my French class. We are all required to go to the blackboard and write some sentences in French, and we are to put our names above our sentences. I have a very distinctive last name. Herb, standing next to me, immediately recognizes it. He knows Craig. I think Herb must be one of Craig's rowdy fraternity brothers, but Herb says no. He and Craig worked at the same radio station in Louisville. I have trouble figuring out how this works because Herb appears to be about my age, and Craig is older. Herb asks to have lunch with me a couple of times. We do lunch, and like each other. Nancy is on alert. Then, Herb asks me out on a date. We are to go bowling with a friend of his and the friend's wife. Wife! I'm eighteen years old and have no thoughts of marriage. What kind of character is this Herb guy?

It just so happens that Craig has come home for the weekend. I ask him about Herb, and he gives me the go ahead to date him. I have no way of telling who is safe and who isn't. Besides, Mom has relied on Craig for years to okay the movies I see, the boys I date, the places I go. Dad isn't interested in that stuff. Craig hasn't seen Herb in a couple of years, but says he's all right.

On the night of the first big date, I am being fitted for a bridesmaid's dress in anticipation of my brother's upcoming wedding. Guess-who is making the dress, and a large assortment of relatives are in the house to meet the bride-elect, as southern newspapers like to say. Therefore, Herb has to run a bit of a gauntlet to get me out of the house. Nancy is fully in charge, Linnie is scared, Tank Girl is oblivious, Ted is quiet because he's looking forward to a trip out of the house. Linda is blissfully unaware that she's four different people.

Eventually, I work up my courage to ask Herb about his married friend. I would see their marriage last longer than our eventual union, and, as far as I know, it continues on to this day. Herb and I embark on a courtship. We are engaged within six months, and say we aren't getting married until we've finished at U of L.

Nancy is so relieved to have the marriage issue settled! She can almost relax now. She doesn't have to meet people any more. Herb's friends become her friends. She quits the sorority, and starts taking classes as fast as possible. Herb wants to go to seminary upon graduation. I have been planning on a career as a teacher in college, but I now adjust my sights to teaching high school because wherever he gets a church there will be a high school. My parents are convinced that I'll never finish school. This is just what they thought would happen: I'd meet some guy and get married. To their surprise, I start taking year-round classes in order to compress my education into three years so I can graduate with Herb who is about a year older than I. I do no extracurricular activities of any sort beyond dating Herb. He has all the ideas for what we do, but I insist on getting the schoolwork done. Years later, he tells our children that he would have never made it through college without me because I was all business when it came to study. I am the second college graduate in the family on Mom's side and the third on Dad's side.

The fly in the ointment comes pretty quickly. Our parents become wildly concerned over our public displays of affection. My parents are certain that Herb and I are having sex. This isn't true—Nancy can't abide the prospect—and she has made it clear to Herb that there are limits to what he can get away with. He thinks I'm just a person of high moral standards. He never recognizes, to my knowledge, the petrified, disgusted little girl who does not trust or wish to be close to anybody. The smells, wetness, the proximity of another body, sweat, bad breath—all that stuff—makes me cringe, makes me nauseous, and this never changes. The reality that my body is just like other adult bodies disgusts me.

A gathering of the clans is held. We are told what we can and cannot do. We protest that we are not doing anything. Skepticism reigns. Herb would like to do more, but he's out of luck. We talk and talk. After a month or two of scrutiny, spying and attempts to control us by our parents, we announce that we are moving up our wedding date and will marry over the Thanksgiving holiday. Everybody immediately starts counting on their fingers. They are certain I am pregnant.

My twenty-five inch waist stays that size for five more years. To the intense wonderment of all, there is no baby and no abortion. Herb and I are simply sick of the hassle. It is easier to be married and finish our last semester and a half than to put up with our parents. Our wedding takes place on an overcast, snow-spitting Thanksgiving Day in Louisville. It is a great inconvenience to all concerned, but Herb doesn't want to take any time off from school or work. Neither do I. He has obtained a "due bill" from a hotel in Chicago. Our room will be free in exchange for advertising on the radio station where he works. The ceremony is at three in the afternoon so that we can quickly get on the road for the six-hour drive to Chicago.

The Zion United Church of Christ, where I am a member,

looks lovely. Herb's parents are florists, so they have made all the decorations and bouquets. My mother has made my dress and two out of three bridesmaids dresses. She has griped about the dresses for months. She thinks we're having a big wedding because I want one. I think it's because she wants one. Her wedding was extremely small, in the backyard of her brother the preacher's parsonage. Her sister-in-law, in the one kind and thoughtful act ever attributed to her, serves cake and lemonade at our wedding. No mention is made of any of Dad's people being there. He has lots of cousins, aunts and uncles in town, but none of them come. Nevertheless, Zion is pretty full. My dress is not frilly or lacy, but it does have a scalloped neckline. I want white velvet, but Mom claims she can't find white velvet, so the dress is peau de soie. I do get to select the bridesmaids' dresses. On their heads, they wear a chrysanthemum tied with a ribbon matching their dresses. It looks kind of stupid, but I'm going to have some say in my wedding plans.

Mom is displaying the wedding gifts at her house. She has insisted that we choose china, crystal and silver patterns. Since she works for the leading department store in Louisville as a buyer, she has loads of contacts and we get full sets of all the dinnerware. Mom says I'm going to be entertaining a lot as a minister's wife, so I need this stuff. I receive, from Mom, a huge punch bowl with a tray and twelve cups. It is crystal, and ends up at more parties than I do. Also, she gives me a fountain syringe. At least she doesn't wrap it as a shower gift. She explains that I'll be needing this, too, but I never know why. She makes me two wool suits for a trousseau and buys a little mink pillbox hat. I get outfitted with some fancy underwear and a nightgown and robe. I get no information regarding what to expect on my wedding night, but I can't hear that from my mother anyway. In our house, we don't talk about sex, we do it. But Nancy has kept me from knowing anything.

On my wedding day, nothing is really different from getting ready for any other dress-up occasion. Mother is starting a turkey. Dad's brother and his wife are there from California; I call him Uncle Stumpy because his leg is in a cast. They've come by train, though it's 1963. President Kennedy is dead—assassinated six days ago. We wonder if we should postpone the wedding on account of it, but, in the end, too many people have come too far for changes to be made. Craig and Rosemary are in from Topeka with a brand-new baby, Michael, so Mom is in her element. She asks Rosemary—I'm not making this up—if they shouldn't give the baby a "little enema" since he hasn't dirtied his diaper in the few hours they've been in the house. Rosemary declines. I stick my head in the hair dryer because I don't need to hear about this.

I'm at loose ends all day. I'm packed for the wedding trip. Most of my belongings are now in my new apartment near Belknap Campus (U of L). Herb and I have collected an amazing assortment of furniture from relatives and a used furniture store. We tried refinishing a maple bookcase that had been in a fire and a table Mom had in the basement. These projects worked out well. We have Herb's bed and dresser, a table and chairs from Aunt Bertie, some living room furniture Aunt Margaret replaced, a TV set Herb repaired. A lot of my joy on that day revolves around the fact that I no longer have to live at home. I think I am crazy in love with Herb, but maybe I'm just filled with the craziness of getting out of jail free after twenty years.

Herb is more than a little nervous. Craig has informed him that if he ever lays a hand on me, he will personally come and kill him. There will be no domestic violence in my marriage. There's not any real worry here as Craig has known Herb longer than I have, and I have been seeing Herb exclusively for a year and a half. Somebody would have noticed a violent streak if there were one. Herb wants to be a Presbyterian minister, which doesn't, of course, exclude him from wife-beating, but does make it less likely. He has not shown any unusual anger, and, being only twenty-one, has not tried much liquor. He never drinks much, and neither do I.

Once when Herb's parents, teetotalers and nonsmokers, come to dinner at my parents' house, Dad asks me to go to the basement refrigerator where extra drinks are kept. "Bring me a Baptist beer," he says. I dutifully return with a beer. He laughs and laughs. He'd meant a soft drink. He laughs, but I think he is embarrassed. He has been informed by Mom that he needs to make a good impression. Herb's parents have tea.

The wedding night fills me with fear. Necking with Herb is one thing, but penetration is another. I believe I am a virgin, though this is highly doubtful. I have successfully blocked out any knowledge. We arrive at our hotel, but it's late. I slip into the silky white gown. I wash my face and brush my teeth. Should I have left my makeup on? I take as much time as I can getting ready. I go to the bathroom, but worry that he might be able to hear me pee. He puts a few moves on me, but I tense up and can't respond. We attribute this to my being tired after the excitement of the day and the long trip. I am so grateful to Herb for letting me off the hook, I can't apologize enough. I am sure that tomorrow will be a different story. So we kiss a little, and go to sleep. Actually, tomorrow never really comes. For four years, I leave the sexual expression part of the marriage completely up to Herb. Nancy goes along with whatever he wants. She never tells him no. She follows his directions in everything. By then, he is graduated from seminary, and has been called to a small church in Clermont County, east of Cincinnati.

The place is a beautiful, small town just like in the movies. The main street runs right through the middle of town with small businesses lining each side. The courthouse and attached jail are a block from the Presbyterian Church. The church, like the town, is old. The building is brick with a sanctuary holding about two hundred. Aged oak woodwork defines the front. The Celtic Cross is in the front, but all the stained glass windows are along either side. Like most Presbyterian churches, First Church is quite plain with carpet on a low dais, lectern and pulpit, two large red-cushioned chairs, choir box and organ. I love its quaintness and the traditions that have been established for years. The congregation couldn't be more friendly and supportive.

We have moved into the manse, a block from the church. The house the church provides for us is huge, Victorian and takes up an entire street corner. The two of us rattle around in it. Herb is into ham radio, so he has one bedroom with his stuff in it. Eventually, he buys a one hundred foot tower, used, which he installs in the back yard. The neighbors think we have some TV antenna! I have my sewing machine in there, too, because there's plenty of room. Closets are everywhere. We also have a guest bedroom in addition to our own bedroom, and an empty room. There are nooks and crannies in the house, and I pick the upstairs nook as a reading area. Downstairs, I put a new cover on the pad of the window seat in the family room, which is another cozy spot. This room has a working fireplace, and was the pastor's study before the church bought the house next to the church and converted it into offices and Sunday School rooms. The room has floor-to-ceiling bookshelves, painted white. When we arrive, we have the furniture we have collected and refinished in Herb's parents' basement, a bed somebody left in the manse, and that's about it. We have to buy some furniture, and the church powers that be give the okay for us to buy some carpets for the downstairs rooms. They also agree to repaint the kitchen celery green from the Pepto-Bismol pink it started out. We put in a little garden in the back yard and trim up the boxwood hedge that runs on the two street sides of the property.

No sooner have we arrived, then the congregation gives us a "pounding." This is an old tradition where the families of the church each give a "pound" of something such as flour, apples, sugar or whatever. They make sure our household is stocked with all the necessary staple foods. They hold a picnic to give the gifts.

As this is Herb's first church, he has to be ordained. He moves his membership from the Louisville Presbytery to the Cincinnati Presbytery. The Presbytery is a geographical association of churches and ministers belong to the Presbytery rather than individual churches. My mother can't be any prouder. Her dreams for me have almost all come true. She merely awaits the inevitable grandchild, which she is certain I will quickly produce. She makes me the inevitable dress for the occasion, and she and Dad come up early to help. The congregation is giving a reception after the ordination, but we will have house guests and visiting dignitaries who will have to have lunch between the morning worship service and the ordination service. I put on my new dress and sit and watch while wonderful things are said about my husband. I am mainly a decoration, a normalizing force that says he's not gay, eccentric or something otherwise off-putting to the congregation. He has a wife, and she is doing just fine looking after him. That is my job—homemaking. I have to be sure he has sufficient clean shirts and socks, meals on the table and a tidy house to come home to when he has a chance.

I have just completed three years of teaching in an inner-city Louisville school, and it bores me to simply take care of the house and laundry. Herb is gone night and day doing good works. He is counseling, preaching, praying over every lunch and supper in the area, joining the Rotary Club, serving on committees, moderating the Session (governing body of an individual church) and on and on. He is never home. I have no car most of the time. He has cautioned me about getting too friendly with any neighbors or members of the congregation because some people will feel left out or think I don't like them, then that will make his job harder. The injunction to love one's neighbor only goes so far. I am frequently distraught because I seem to have no purpose in life. He grudgingly takes me along to meetings and so on, just to shut me up. Nancy is accustomed to constant struggle, and this seems small potatoes to her. She also spends much time alone, so interactions with others are not likely to trip the switch that leads to Linnie, Ted or Tank Girl. Herb is so full of himself and his importance, he doesn't notice any problem. He just thinks I'm being silly and immature when I get upset because he's always out.

Linnie is well- hidden now that I no longer live with my parents. She drifts back behind her rock. While Nancy is handling the sexual duties, Linnie keeps to herself. She is squashed beneath the social role that Nancy plays so well. Ted is squelched because he is so apt to say something inappropriate, and after the first few times Herb chews me out for making a smart aleck remark or, for heaven's sake, saying something about myself, Ted sneaks back into the shadows. I pretty much stop talking altogether. Tank Girl is serene through all this. She never comes out anyway.

I don't want to teach school, but I agree to substitute. We decide we should have a baby. The congregation is kind of looking forward to it as there has not been a baby in the manse for some forty years.

I'm excited, but ignorant. I know what I have to do in order to get pregnant, but it isn't Nancy's favorite pastime to lie around in bed with Herb. She likes him, but she likes playing mommies more—just like we used to play with Betty Ann or Jeanie Ellen or one of the other dolls. Of course, the doll is missing so far.

Becoming pregnant is no easy task. After about a year of trying, we are no closer to the goal. So, I go scientific. I take my temperature every morning. I call Herb to come home in the middle of the day, if necessary. He is delighted. "You are sure more sexy when you want to have a baby," he says. He is right. I have virtually no interest in sex except for right now. One cold day in January, something clicks. It is, however, well into February before I have enough clues to consult a doctor. My information on pregnancy has been confined to the Hollywood version, and I am neither morning-sick nor prone to fainting. I don't even know that my periods will stop. That is what tips me off that there might be something going on, and, thanks to my reading campaign, I know to consult the doctor.

At age twenty-four, I have my second-ever pelvic exam. I am scared out of my senses and have a lot of trouble relaxing enough for the doctor to look at me. My usual stress symptoms start up—clammy hands, churning stomach, inability to focus on reality, need to use the bathroom, an intense desire to run away. I sweat in the waiting room, scared to death somebody I know will come in—this is a very small town, and I am now a prominent citizen by virtue of being Herb's wife. When I get into the examining room, I nearly pass out. Of course, I'm going to have to take off my clothes and don a hospital gown. By the time I'm on the table—my feet aren't even in the stirrups yet—Nancy smoothly steps in and handles the doctor situation. I am poised, matter-of-fact, calm. All my symptoms leave. "It's a little early to tell by looking," the doctor says, "but I'd say you're pregnant. You'll need to get a urine test at the lab to be sure."

After Nancy is dressed, she sits in front of the doctor's desk to hear him ask a few questions and give her some information. He calculates the due date on a two-piece circular card which reminds Nancy a little of the slide rule we used in physics class back in high school or a grade calculator that we've seen teachers use. "September 30th," he declares. No foods or activities (except horseback riding) are limited. I am not sick. I should rest if I feel tired and eat saltines if I'm nauseous, and call him a couple of days after I visit the lab. I go home and tell Herb, but we agree to tell no one else until we're sure. Telling my mother never enters my mind, although she has refrained fairly well from nagging me about getting pregnant. She is more than ready for a third grandchild, especially since she could probably get her hands on my child. Craig lives in Chicago now.

A few days later, the lab report comes back. We've succeeded! Do we now call all the relatives? No indeed. We know we will have to inform them, but we are going to wait as long as we can. The MBS—Mom Broadcasting System—will do the job, but we are ecstatic, planning already and deciding which of our four upstairs bedrooms will be the nursery. The empty room is near the master bedroom, so we choose it for the nursery. I know right away that I am not going to want to trek up and down stairs all day to tend to the baby, so we plan to put a small crib and changing table in our enormous dining room which measures about nineteen feet long and fifteen feet wide. I plan to get a plastic tub to bathe the baby in because my family tradition of using the kitchen sink isn't even a consideration for me.

I've actually been using the dining room for entertaining. Right from the start, Herb has been inviting all the groups from the church over for dinner. The Session comes. We have open house, the youth group has meetings at our house, and we have out-of-town guests frequently. Nancy is constantly in the throes of planning some event, cooking for it or cleaning up after it. We are asked to house a Peace Corps volunteer for three weeks or so. She is to find out what "rural" life is like before she goes to some third-world place to build a dam or something. This, to me, is an absolute hoot. This kid comes from Denver. It amazes her to watch me bake cookies because I do not need to use a timer. After thousands of batches of cookies, I just know about when to get them out of the oven. Somebody gives me a lot of strawberries, so, much to her astonishment, I make jam. Few foods are easier to produce. We point out things that are two hundred or more years old in the neighborhood. She's never seen so many deciduous trees in her life. I think she has a good time. Now, I wonder if all the entertaining and visitors are going to continue.

In mid-March, we drive to Louisville for a Friday-Saturday weekend. Herb has to preach Sunday, so we can't stay, which is fine with Nancy and me. My parents invite his parents over for dinner, and while we are washing dishes, my mother says, "When are you going to have a baby?"

"September," I answer. The shocked silence is gratifying.

"What?" my mother and mother-in-law chorus in unison.

"That's what the doctor said—September 30th."

They forget all about me. I keep clearing the table, and my mother says, "Well, Dorothy, the nightgown did it!" She is very pleased with herself.

"What nightgown?" I say.

"That frilly blue one I gave you for Christmas. It worked. I knew it would."

I am so annoyed! Now Mom is taking credit for getting me pregnant! She has no idea, and will never have any idea, what an effort I made to have this child. She babbles on, wondering if six months will give her enough time to dress me and the baby. She is determining where the baby furniture will come from, wants to know how I'm decorating the nursery. I have given it some thought, but nothing has been done. I've been pregnant about ten weeks. I don't even need maternity clothes yet. Dorothy, my mother-in-law, is pretty well steamrollered like I am. She doesn't say much, but she gives me a hug and congratulates me. This will be her very first grandchild. We finish the dishes. Herb is informing our fathers of the situation.

When I enter the room later, I don't remember my father saying anything, but he smiles when my father-in-law congratulates me. I don't realize that my in-laws are the normal people here. I love them, and feel more comfortable with them than with my own family, but I don't know why. Herb is their eldest child, so at this time, they still have his siblings living at home. That's why we stay with my parents overnight—they have more room. Dad has lost interest in me for the most part, but perhaps he sees a glimmer of hope—my baby could be a girl.

Mom is a clothing buyer for the department store now. She buys casual dresses and uniforms, which necessitates frequent trips out of town. She goes to New York several times a year to see the new lines, and to schmooze with the vendors. Now I start getting smocks and loose dresses from the vendors who are hoping Mom will buy more and more stuff. Her contacts in the local store put her on to bargains in maternity wear and baby wear, so I'm collecting quite a closet full. I am careful to report only that the doctor says I'm fine. This is true. I do not mention my concerns about actually giving birth, and they are legion.

Just before my niece is born (about two years earlier), Mom tells me that she hopes the baby will be a girl since Craig and Rosemary already have the little boy. When I remark, "That will be up to Craig," she doesn't know what I am talking about. I have to explain to her that the sperm is the determiner of gender, that eggs are all female, so it's the X or the Y chromosome that makes the difference. This is news to her.

"Why are there so many years between Craig and me?" I innocently ask.

"Oh, your Dad didn't want a second child. I always thought you were lucky to be a girl and to look like his people."

I am stunned. Somewhere inside, I realize that I'm not wanted, especially by Dad. As I ponder this, years later, I figure out that I am a trick pulled on Dad—a fast one, as it were. I have one letter that my Mom sent to her mother not long after Craig was born. It is highly upbeat, suspiciously so when I consider the things she has said about this period of her life. She is lonely, living in Long Beach, California, on the Navy base, miles and cultural light years away from everything familiar. I am now starting to understand the deal. I wonder why Leland married her or why she married him. She was nineteen years old, just out of school, had a good job, and, theoretically, access to any eligible bachelor in Louisville. She wanted to be somebody. Leland's sister, her best friend, had died. She really didn't have to connect to that family at all anymore. So, I wonder if they had a sexual relationship before he went off to the Navy, and somehow felt pressured to get married. I can see this from her point of view, but not his. He was clearly not concerned about virginity or moral standards.

They are married in 1936. Craig arrives in late 1937, but I don't make an appearance until late 1943. This seems strange when I think that most families tended to have stair-step children just two or three years apart.

I surmise that Dad doesn't like Craig from the outset, despite Mom's letter describing him as "beaming with pride and joy" when he sees the cooing, gurgling three-month-old while home for the weekend. Sailors cruise. That's what they do for weeks at a time. Mom is alone with Craig, who has his problems since he does not read the Navy doctors' instructions for the care and feeding of infants carefully. Had Craig read them, he might have understood better that babies are to be fed on a strict four- hour schedule. If they get hungry and cry for an hour or two, that's okay. If, when they're fed, they are too exhausted to eat the full meal, that's tough. If they then fall asleep for an hour and wake up hungry, well, they can't be fed again for two hours. I ask my mother why she didn't just feed the kid when he was hungry.

"The Navy doctors wouldn't take care of him if I didn't follow the schedule."

"So why didn't you just lie to them? I wouldn't put up with that."

The Navy's no-nonsense approach to child-rearing resounds on down to me to some extent. I lose bottle privileges at nine months of age. Since Craig has been attached to a blanket, and Mom doesn't like it, I have no special toy or blanket. If pacifiers have been invented, I don't know about it. A baby could cry its heart out in our house and the solution to the problem was paregoric, usually. I have a disgusting penchant for projectile vomiting, but manage to quit just before surgery is recommended. Babies as young human beings are not a priority in our home. I think I am conceived as a distracter for Dad, to divert his energy away from Craig. The reason I'm lucky to be a girl is that I am spared the rage and beating. Apparently the sexual abuse is okay. I am profoundly angry at my mother, but not while she's alive. I am, to some degree, dependent still, still terrified of her and still wanting to distance myself from her.

When the birth of my baby arrives, I have no clear notion of what's going to happen. The part I am most afraid of is not pain or indignity, but the enema I know I'm getting when I have to go to the hospital. I understand that it is highly unlikely that a first child will be born in a hurry, so there'll be plenty of time for all kinds of "preparation." In fact, it is three weeks before my due date. I am thoroughly worn out from cleaning the house (including a new rug for the nursery), shopping for a rocker and a toy chest, cooking a big dinner and washing the dishes. I have gotten my bulky self into bed, and am dozing off. Herb is watching TV—the Reds are playing on the West Coast, so the game starts late in Ohio. Suddenly, I am riveted by a feeling of great tension below what used to be my waist. I can't figure out what's causing this. Should I go to the bathroom? I just urinated a few minutes ago. I lay there for a while pondering the situation when all at once a warm flood gushes out from between my legs. It doesn't feel like urination, but just what it is does not register. I call for Herb and tell him to turn on the light. I am afraid I'm having a hemorrhage, but, no. The bed is wet, but it isn't blood. It's more like urine, but I know my bladder is empty. I'm still leaking, so I go to the bathroom anyway to spare the mattress more insult. Herb calls the doctor. The doctor is at a party—this is Saturday night. He explains to Herb that my water has broken and I will start into labor within twenty-four hours. He says that when the pains are ten minutes apart, we should head for the hospital because it's a thirty-mile drive along mostly two-lane roads.

We wait a couple of hours. I seem to have stopped dripping, but I'm having a few cramps now and then. The cramps escalate to some pinching pains. We really don't know what to do or what to expect, so about three or four in the morning, we decide we'd better go on to the hospital. Herb calls one of the elders of the church, tells him we're going, and that the liturgy for tomorrow's service will be in our mailbox. This is the one Sunday in September that Herb does not have to preach. A missionary on furlough has been scheduled.

All the way to the hospital, I am scared. Nancy has a little trouble overcoming Linnie, who always appears at times like this. Linnie is the fearful one, the terrorized one, the helpless one, the baby. When we get in the hospital and all the "preparations" go on, Nancy remains in control. We look and sound like any ordinary patient. We ask no questions except one: "What is this pill going to do?" The answer is, "The doctor ordered it." Years later, I determine that it was probably Seconal used in the hopes of stopping premature labor. Nancy takes the pill without fuss because she has her hands full with Linnie. We go to sleep. The nurses send Herb home where he gets in about an hour's nap before they call him to come back. It looks like the baby's coming, no matter what. I am doped up enough not to be too concerned about the number of people investigating my bare bottom. The pain itself feels like the cramps I've had for years, and they never become the crushers I'll experience later with my other children. Finally, late in the afternoon, I'm rolled into the delivery room and placed on the table. I'm given a saddle block, so now I don't feel anything. The drugs are wearing off.

"Do you want to watch?" the doctor asks.

"Yes," Nancy answers. Now that the pain is gone, she is curious to see what will happen next. The doctor sets a mirror where we can see the whole thing.

"Looks like a girl's head. I'm going to use the forceps here, just to guide the baby. I'll have to cut you just a little bit. Well! It's a girl!"

I have eyes only for my tiny baby daughter. Nurses are swishing her around, cleaning her off, weighing and measuring her, getting an Apgar score, wrapping her up. I can't believe I've had a baby, but there she is. Am I overwhelmed with joy? Well, yes and no. I now have someone to keep me company when Herb is gone, but I also can't just put Laura (that's the name we've chosen) in a dresser drawer if she gets to be a hassle. I've already made up my mind that there are some things she's never going to experience if I can help it. I am not able to articulate what those things will be. I just know that she will be raised differently from me.

September 9, 1968. I am lying in my hospital bed resting up from giving birth the previous evening. I lost a lot of blood and received a transfusion, but am still feeling anemic. The phone rings next to my bed. It is my mother, and she is not happy. She is calling from New York where she is on a buying trip, and if she had known I was in labor, she would have cancelled the trip and come straight to Cincinnati instead. She is disappointed to have missed the medical drama. Furthermore, she didn't even get the message from Dad (Herb called him) until too late to call last night. I am unrepentant, and an accomplished liar.

"Well, Mom, we really didn't know she was coming. I thought that since it was so early, they'd just send me back home." This seems to mollify her. I describe the baby, but I leave out the part where she looks so much like my own baby pictures it's unnerving. Mom will be at my house the day after I come home. She just can't possibly get to Cincinnati any sooner. "Don't rush." I tell her, "We'll manage." I don't mention that I'm trying to breastfeed, but it isn't going well. Mom disapproves of breastfeeding on the grounds that nobody knows exactly how much the baby's eating. Laura has no interest in food anyway at this point, but I still think she'll catch on. She likes to look at the lights, and she's really small—less than six pounds. I'm afraid the pediatrician won't let me take her home right away.

Scars

The scars are tender yet where
The deep gashes sliced through my soul
And laid it open.

When you touch those marks, I wince,
Hurting still, and yet so moved
That you care enough to touch
And help the healing.

Sometimes, I see the scars you hide so well,
And wonder if they are still tender,
Like mine.

Let me stretch out my hand,
And, so gently,
Touch you.

abies take time. By the time I've fed, bathed, dressed the baby and put her down for a nap, I need a nap myself. There's not a moment of the day that I'm thinking about anything except my daughter and her father. Nancy is the epitome of small town motherhood. We get a baby carriage and dress Laura up for rides around town. It's just like playing with Jeanie Ellen or Betty Ann, but Laura's warm and responsive. She lets me know if things are not going to suit her. Her diapers are really wet and dirty. Her daddy is not very willing to take care of her when it means dealing with anything unpleasant, although he really enjoys showing her off. I get up with her at night, take her to the doctor at the specified intervals. She is healthy, and I don't look for symptoms. I fully believe I'm living.

Herb is more and more involved in small group dynamics and various versions of "touchy-feely" encounter groups. I am highly uncomfortable with this and feel left out. He is gone sometimes for a week at a time, and when he comes home, he's drunk on emotion. Some of his friends, another minister's wife, in particular, call me and try to persuade me that everything he's doing is fine and I should try to be more accepting. I do try, but Linnie is scared, and besides, this is not what I signed on for.

When Herb is at seminary, I belong to a wives' club called "Divinity Dames." The whole concept gives me a crawling, want-to-retch kind of feeling, but in the early '60s, not many women attend seminary to become pastors. There is, I believe, one woman in Herb's graduating class. Although there is no prohibition about women becoming pastors in the Presbyterian church, not very many do. Women are to serve with their husbands as unpaid assistants-teaching Sunday School, running youth groups, cooking, baking, serving dinners and parties for the congregations, singing in the choir, running off the bulletins, taking an active part in the women's groups, being a leader in the community (in a wifely sort of way), taking in strays, doing good works and so on ad infinitum. The Divinity Dames function as a kind of training bra for fledglings. Wives of the professors (a woman theologian—laughable!) meet with us sweet young things and teach us the ropes.

Can we pour tea sitting down? As if to the manor born. Do we know to put a doily under the cookies? Absolutely. Do we know what to do when some woman in the congregation makes googly eyes at our husband? Well, no, but one experienced wife points out, "You wouldn't want something that nobody else wanted, would you?" I gather I should be above it all. My man is so fabulous that I'll just have to learn to share him with all the ladies of the congregation. It wouldn't be Christian to expect otherwise. This serves to reinforce the sense I have already developed, almost to full capacity, that I am worthless. I am to keep house, to focus on "kinder, kirch and kuchen"—children, church and kitchen. We learn to make "reformatory cake," which is simple, but surprisingly good. It is angel food cake, split in half, a trench about an inch or so wide dug out, mixed with prepared whipped cream and thawed frozen strawberries, reconstructed, coated with more of the whipped cream stuff, and decorated with a few fresh strawberries. It's called "reformatory cake" because once a month several of us make the cake and it is taken out to the LaGrange Reformatory to celebrate the inmates' birthdays for that month.

We try out desserts and hors d'oeuvres on each other. We discuss how to lead discussions. We share tips on bargain-hunting. At one point, my mother comes and runs a fashion show for us. We're the models. The professors' wives are a wealth of stories and helpful hints. We organize activities for couples living on campus. We talk about field assignments—our husbands all have jobs with churches or hospital chaplaincy on weekends. Herb and I leave after school on Fridays, drive to Harrodsburg, Kentucky, and stay all weekend, coming home after youth group on Sunday night. We leave our pet parakeet, Beau Beau (short for Beauregard), with our seminary neighbors because we're afraid he'll be too lonely without us. We also have a twenty gallon fish tank in our apartment. Laura is not born yet. She comes along during Herb's first pastorate.

I spend some time in Harrodsburg with the wife of the installed pastor there who is Herb's supervisor. The church rents us a room in someone's home for the first year, but in the second year, they fix up a two-room apartment in a building they own next door to the church. I sing in the church choir on Sundays, make lesson plans for my classes at the high school where I teach and make youth group plans. We help with church camp, Vacation Bible School, Herb preaches once in a while. In general, we practice our future roles. We get invited to fine dinners in beautiful old homes in this quiet town about forty miles from Lexington. These well-heeled families, usually older people, have maids and cooks whom they summon by means of a bell system under the table, usually in the floor. Now all those Sunday dinners Mom made pay off. I may have been dazzled by the display, but I could eat anything set before me. Thanks to Divinity Dames, I could converse appropriately. Nancy's ability to read people keeps me from messing up too badly, but Herb starts his lifelong campaign to keep me from embarrassing him and ruining his career. Every action and word become subject to his scrutiny. I am admonished daily regarding what I should and shouldn't say or do. I do not think my own thoughts-I don't know what they are. Mom continues to dress me and make sure I collect the punch bowls, teacups and linens she is sure I'll need. Divinity Dames explains all the church situations, and Herb provides ongoing advice. I can't be trusted to handle anything on my own. I even require supervision to cook and clean.

Herb teaches me to drive, but I am not allowed to drive. I ride to school with four other seminary wives, two Presbyterian and two Baptist (the Louisville Baptist Seminary is located less than a mile from the Presbyterian). We take turns driving until I sideswipe a telephone pole. I am stopped at the time, but don't realize I am against the pole until I pull out of a drive into traffic. Nothing is hurt but the car, however, my driving days are once more over. In the car, we all talk the talk. We seldom see each other at school because the school is large. We discuss recipes primarily, and how hard our husbands work. One wife asks every day what we are fixing for supper. She discovers something she calls tomato "pure," which she likes to put in just about everything. This is the same woman who puts an entire cup of baking soda in a cher-ry cobbler and is astounded at all the places cherry cobbler can run. She has problems with pizza from a box mix, so we spend a lot of time giving her explicit instructions.

We are all living in one of the most prestigious areas of Louisville. The Presbyterian Seminary adjoins Cherokee Park, and is designed to fit into the surrounding trees and huge, gorgeous homes set well back off the streets around the park. The seminary grounds feature a valley separating the housing area from the school buildings. Nothing but green lawn and old trees mark the seminary from the entrance gate for at least a quarter of a mile. On the other side—at that time, the University of Louisville's music school—Gardencourt rambles across a couple of acres. I take voice lessons there briefly.

Our brand-new apartment consists of one large room. The building is motel-style. We have one picture window. There is a study area for Herb, and a fairly large closet. The kitchen is in the end of the room by the door. We have moved from a four-room apartment into this furnished place. We sleep on a sofa-bed, so if Herb studies late, I have to sleep with the light on. We invest in a screen to put beside the door to create a kind of entry way, so that people don't just walk into the room. We are crammed in there five days a week, then gone every weekend. It is intense. I end up hav-ing to help Herb with his studying. He has over four hundred index cards with facts about church history on each side. On the way to the field, I quiz him from the cards. I type better and faster than he does, so I have to type all his papers, including his exegeses for his Greek and Hebrew classes. I have to leave blank spaces for him to write in the Greek and Hebrew characters. Of course, I have my own work to do. I have five classes a day of inner city junior high students. One class has thirty-nine students, and I have five preparations because, even though these students are ostensibly using the same curriculum, they are varied in their academic levels. If I have the top class, I also have the bottom class. Since I am teaching English, I have papers to assign and grade. I am teaching novels and plays and writing. I like my students, but two of them are pregnant, a situation not covered in my college classes.

To add to the mix, I am one of a hundred twenty-two teachers in this combined junior-senior high. One day in the teachers' lounge, I hear another teacher lamenting that she needs a certain magazine for her distributive education class. This is a magazine my mother receives, so I tell the teacher I can get her some copies. She is thrilled. When I bring them in, she asks if I can get out of homeroom to bring them up to her classroom. "I'll write a note to your teacher," she says. "No," I tell her, "I am the teacher." I then send the magazines up by one of my students.

The Civil Rights Movement is in full swing, this being the early '60s. The seminary is involved, but Herb and I stay out of the whole thing. I think he is a little afraid of getting arrested or hurt. I am not thrilled by that idea either. Besides, I am trying every day to help African-American students get the same education as my white students, and I like them. I think I'm doing my part. My parents continue to be astounded that I can teach in the inner city, that I don't get mugged, that my African-American students appear to like me. Of course, Mom and Dad are still surprised to see black people in the Blue Boar Cafeteria, at the movies and in hospitals. They are adjusting to reality slowly, and I think I am helping them to understand that skin color is the difference; otherwise, we are all striving for an even ground. I believe that any of my students can be successful. This is about as worked up as Nancy can get about anybody else's troubles. I am unaware of Nancy, Linnie, Ted and Tank Girl. My schedule is so hectic, and so is Herb's, that I am not able to think about how I feel.

On the long drives to the field, Herb discusses various moral dilemmas, theological points and philosophies with me. I believe I have a grasp of these ideas, but they are completely external and intellectual. Due to my basic mistrust of others, my wish to be left alone and my relief at being out of my parents' grip (all this is out of my awareness), I profess a live-and-let-live philosophy. I am not eager to convert sinners or even identify them. I am not qualified to determine someone else's moral state.

Herb, on the other hand, feels compelled to take the Gospel to the ends of the Earth—at least to Harrodsburg and Pleasant Grove, Kentucky—where, in fact, the Good News is pretty much old news, given that these churches have been established for far longer than either Herb or I have been alive. He is wrapped up in the problems of others and trying to provide spiritual help from his books and professors, rather than experience. He has had a great time at church camp, too. I am simply trying to cope with pregnant eighth-graders who nearly give birth in my classroom, kids who steal from the bakery truck because nobody feeds them and kids who don't get their report cards signed for four or five weeks because their parents work odd hours and don't even see the kid every day. I inhabit two worlds—the work-week world of poverty and need and the weekend world of uniformed maids delivering meals worthy of *Gourmet* magazine just after a well-dressed crowd of white people sing three or four songs about Jesus and listen to my husband or his equivalent tell them nice theological ideas. I just accept this as normal, but then, what is normal to me?

My two worlds regularly clash, but I seldom notice. I live in Nancyland. I am sorry for people who have trouble, but don't see how I can do much about it. I don't like to get advice, so I don't give any either. I adapt myself to the circumstances as best I can and creep off into the woodwork as much as possible. Ironically, since I have better teaching skills than Herb, I end up planning a lot of programs and activities which he presents while I sit adoringly in the crowd accepting compliments on his behalf. "Why that's the best program we've ever had on ___________!" "He certainly knows how to get a point across!"

I want some credit, too, but I don't get it. I'm the "little woman" behind the great man, and as far as I know, that's all I'll ever be. I've had a brief reprieve in high school where I was very active in clubs and organizations, popular with my teachers, and the possessor of several close friends, but I did not feel like one of them. Mom liked the idea that I was a leader, but she preferred it be my brother. I wrote a poem one time which she thought for years had been written by Craig. She would have continued to think that if she hadn't been cleaning out a box of old papers, and thought to ask somebody. Even when I told her the circumstances, and despite the fact that I wrote a weekly column for a county newspaper at the time, she still had to ask me several times, and check with Craig as well, to be sure I'd written this silly little poem about our family gatherings. I was editor of the high school newspaper, accepting awards on behalf of it, traveling to journalism conventions in New York City, my picture running weekly with the county paper column, and my mother wasn't sure who wrote this poem.

Married to Herb, I am more subdued than ever. He keeps picking up helpful hints for me. I am never to talk about myself or tell any story about my experience because this takes the focus off the other person. I am to use the counseling techniques he is being taught in my conversation. I am to listen, not speak. It is okay for me to go to Divinity Dames, but it is not okay for me to go to the movies with anyone except Herb, and he will select the film. I can read anything I want as long as I don't mention it. If I get a phone call, he needs to know who it is and needs to monitor the conversation. I lose touch with all my high school friends, and I have made no friends in college because I began to date Herb within a few weeks of arriving back home. This does not strike me as odd. My whole life has been geared to being one person at home and another in public. My sense of humor is too warped for Herb as well. I am accustomed to constant ridicule, so I am adept at sarcasm, the smart remark and the inappropriate comment. Now that I hang around with church people all the time, I have to keep myself in check. The first time I hear the term "flaming asshole," I am shocked. I have probably heard it a million times, but Nancy has kept that information away from me. I am a non-smoker, a non-drinker and a well-known prude. I don't like myself at all. I have no escapades to report. I am dull, stupid and boring, but I can cook and sew.

I Don't Understand

I don't understand the whys.
They prick at me in the dark soft places
And hammer where my armor still fits.
Such a variety of little evils
Picking, picking, picking away,
Deviling my mind and reminding
My body of all it is trying to forget.
The battle cry continues:
"Who knew? Why didn't they stop him?"
Only a hollow whisper answers:
"I don't know."

Eight

When I start to remember the abuse, one of the first needs I have is to try to understand my spiritual life. Having been connected to the church for my entire life, I know that this is an important area of exploration for me. My therapist is not equipped to handle spirituality to the depth I'm going to require. My life is a lie. I have been somebody else for over forty years, so I have to find out who professed a belief in Jesus Christ as Lord and Savior, who prayed, who did good works, who was a pastor's wife for eighteen years. Is that who I am? Do I believe all that or any of it any more? I have to wonder what God thinks about all of it, and God doesn't seem forthcoming on the subject.

As a small child, I go to church most Sundays, but I spend the time in the nursery. All I remember about that is the baby gate across the door, and my mother stopping by after church to say that she'd be picking me up after she went to the "rest" room. I picture a darkened room full of beds. I think it strange to have adults taking naps in special rooms at the church when we aren't there that long to begin with. After a while, I ask to be taken along. I want to see this place!

I know better than to register my surprise or indicate that it was anything I have misconceived. I dutifully use the "rest" room, which pleases Mom. I learn to do the finger play, "Here is the church. Here is the steeple. Open the doors, and see all the people." On occasion, I go into the "big" church. It's pretty boring, but my mother does try to teach me to sing the hymns.

Memories of church when I was very small include standing between my parents singing "America, the Beautiful" and refusing to sing the line "And crown thy good with brotherhood" because I am mad at Craig. I am dragged along to the "Faith, Fun and Fellowship" couples group, which probably met once a month for a potluck dinner and program. My father called the group "Fat, Flatulent and Forty." I take a toy and run wild with some other kids in a separate room from the adults. I don't recall any supervision. Children are allowed to leave the worship service when communion is served, and we are rebuked soundly about making too much noise outside the open church windows in the summer. There is an annual church picnic with glass-bottled soft drinks in tubs of ice and nine kinds of potato salad. The most glorious part of the picnic is playing on the playground without parental interference.

Dad has to work a lot of Sundays, so there are plenty of times when we don't go to church. I learn to sing in Sunday School, and to bring the same number of pennies as I am years old for a special offering on my birthday. I hear Bible stories and make crafts. I think Miss Esther likes me. I can draw on the bulletin or read the little Sunday School paper I get each week during the worship service. My dad serves communion because he is on the church board, stays after to help count the money and takes some responsibility for the church.

My parents are friends with the pastor and his wife. This is a situation I have never really understood. It must be the women who are the friends because Dad has virtually nothing in common with the pastor who is a slightly built man, very quiet and, well, pastoral. Perhaps it is a true friendship or maybe it is a social-climbing exercise, but we even go on vacation with these people. They have a daughter about a year or so older than Craig, whom I adore. She plays paper dolls with me sometimes, and will let me play with her baby dolls, too, long after she's outgrown them. She and Craig are friends and have mutual friends that they run around with, so when we visit, frequently, I'm the only child who actually stays at the house. This is no problem as I have the dolls. I think my parents play cards with the pastor and his wife, but not any gambling games. The pastor's wife is exceedingly traditional. My mother is quite shocked when the pastor's daughter gets the marriage and baby sequence reversed.

At this time in my life, church is simply social. Sure, we sing songs and memorize Bible verses, and color pictures of Jesus blessing the children, but the real theological education comes later. I'm sure they have Vacation Bible School, but I don't go because my mother doesn't drive, doesn't have a car and we have moved across town from the church. Not too long after the pastor's daughter creates her scandal, the pastor and his wife move on to another state and another church. We move along, too.

When I reach about sixth grade, my parents decide we should change churches. My dad has family connections in most of the Evangelical and Reformed Churches in town and the new one, Zion, is located just outside an area in Louisville known as "Schnitzelburg" due to the large number of German immigrants who populate the area. Many of these people are related to Dad because his mother is one of seventeen children (she was number sixteen), so she has people all over the area. They all belong to the E &R church. I never am introduced to many of Dad's relatives. I only know my aunts, uncles and two cousins, but none of them well because none of them lives anywhere nearby. I knew my mother's Christian Church relatives.

Zion Church is filled with distant cousins of my dad, but it makes no difference to me. I immediately get involved in Sunday School and the Lightbearer's Choir. The Lightbearer's Choir is good-sized. This church is much larger than the old one. To join the choir, each child has to learn the pledge and recite it weekly: "As a member of the Lightbearer's Choir, I promise I will be faithful in attendance, reverent in worship and diligent in learning music that will help bring people closer to God." There is a theme song: "We would be along the way, bearers of the light. Turning night to brightest day, bearers of the light. Light of Jesus we would bear, with the world its glory share. Bringing brightness everywhere, bearers of the light." The Bible verse is Matthew 5:16: "Let your light so shine before men, that they may see your good works and give glory to your Father who is in heaven." We have to memorize that, too. We meet from 11:00 to 12:00 every Saturday morning in the church "parlor" where there is a big grand piano. Every kind of musical talent is encouraged. Miss Elsie, the church organist and choir director, also directs the Cherub Choir made up of children third grade and under. We make reports on composers, give theological interpretations of the lyrics to everything we sing, learn to sing in harmony and memorize everything. It is an excellent choir. We sing with the adult choir from time to time, and on our own. We have robes. We learn to watch

Miss Elsie whether she is at the organ or the piano. Some of the kids take piano lessons from her as well. We are amazingly well-behaved. Nobody wants Miss Elsie calling his or her parents to find out why we aren't at practice or why we don't follow directions. If you are in the choir, you are in the choir. Mom even tries out the adult choir, but has trouble getting to rehearsals or something, so she stops. I ride the bus on Saturdays.

The very next school year is a critical one spiritually. In seventh grade, we are confirmed, taking on for ourselves the responsibility of the baptismal vows our parents had, presumably, made for us as infants. This taking of responsibility is not viewed as any superficial exercise. For the entire nine months of the school year, we meet from 9:00 on Saturday mornings until 11:00, at which time most of us go to choir. Our classes open with worship—we girls take turns playing the hymns on the piano—and proceed with lecture, discussion, note-taking and testing. We have a catechism to memorize, the Apostle's Creed, the Lord's Prayer, the Gloria Patri and several other items. We read the Bible, discuss the finer points of the meaning and rules of church membership and are encouraged to think about our future as leaders in the congregation.

We each have to pass a six-page written test, as well as an oral test before the congregation, and learn a memory verse to repeat to the pastor at the time of confirmation. We are cautioned that, although we have each been assigned a question to answer at the oral exam, the congregation is free to ask us any question they like, and they can vote against our becoming members if they don't like what they hear. As there are over thirty children in my class, this is highly unlikely to happen, but we are warned all the same. Becoming a church member is no lightly undertaken activity. A few kids have to be baptized, but the great majority of us have the baptismal certificates and the church records to show that we are "kingdom kids."

The confirmation process occupies the two weeks before Easter and Easter Sunday, itself. On the first Sunday, we appear in church in our white robes. We process in behind the choir and take our reserved seats in the left-hand section, front four pews. All the girls wear white satin ribbons. One by one, we advance to the microphone in the center of the chancel and answer our catechism questions. I remember being nervous, but getting out my answer acceptably. No one in the congregation asks any questions, but a few make comments about what a well-prepared class and what a fine class we are.

Palm Sunday, the week before Easter, we are actually confirmed. I have new dresses for all these occasions, even though I wear a white robe each Sunday. All of the candidates wear white carnations on the robes. It is rumored that Reverend Kohler does not have to confirm a person who does not know his or her memory verse. When a child gets to the kneeler, he or she is to whisper the memory verse to the pastor, and if he thinks it is satisfactory, he will proceed with the confirmation. I go up to the front scared. I have practiced my verse over and over, but it is really two verses: Matthew 10:32-33: "So everyone who acknowledges me before men, I also will acknowledge before my Father who is in heaven; but who ever denies me before men, I also will deny before my Father who is in heaven." I have been impressed with the fact that this is no idle choice for a memory verse. It is chosen particularly for me, although I don't grasp the reason. I guess it looks to Reverend Kohler as if I might be one to keep quiet about my faith—not entirely inaccurate. When he places his hand on my head to confirm me, I feel a peculiar rush. It is a sexual rush, but I don't recognize it as such. I feel a shiver go through me, confusing me, making me wonder whether I want it to stop or not. Perhaps it is something spiritual, but I can't explain it. I have to be helped to my feet from my knees, and I don't remember anything else about the day except wearing a pink-and-black-checked pinafore-type jumper. I know there is a party after church at home, and lots of relatives are there. I get a watch from my parents and a Bible with my name in gold from the church. I feel mature more than excited, and serious more than joyous about my confirmation. The classes have made me question a lot of religious teachings, and I am just beginning to try to figure out what it all means.

On Easter, the confirmation class receives communion for the first time. This is huge, and we are convinced in every way of the solemnity of the occasion. Salvation, obviously, doesn't arrive on a silver platter for just anyone to sample. Whoever said "Work out your own salvation with fear and trembling" must have been a founder of the E & R tradition. In preparation for this feast, our minister has told us that this might be the only time in our lives that we will receive communion from the minister himself (there is no such animal as the minister herself). Though we don't have to worry about dropping anything—we are being served bread and grape juice as symbols of the body and blood of Jesus—nevertheless, we must be reverent, awed and, above all, careful! It is to be a magical, spiritual moment where we take God into ourselves. We will be changed by the experience. My experience turns out to be that of eating a cube of white bread and washing it down with less than a thimbleful of Welch's. Jesus chooses not to make a second coming that day.

Many of my questions about religion come from Ted. As we move into adolescence, he appears more often with his defiance and wisecracks. We attend Sunday School, worship, Youth Fellowship and Youth Choir now. In all of those events, Bible study is an important element. I start besetting the youth leaders with question after question. Where did Cain and Abel get wives? Why is God so big on smiting in the Old Testament? If God sees every sparrow that falls, why do people think they can get away with stuff? Why is there evil? Is Satan a real entity? If these people can bring it up, I can ask about it. I usually get the party line on this because our youth leaders tend to be seminary students from the Presbyterian Seminary (the same one Herb will attend), and they really don't have much more experience than I do. They are never more than about eight years older than I am. I am not trying to be difficult, but my life is not matching the pattern provided by the church. To me, most of Christian teaching thoroughly defies logic, yet there do not seem to be logical explanations available.

I don't have, I discover, the traditional foundations for Christian belief. I, of course, at the subconscious level, have no model of a good parent. The parenting I receive is hypocritical, and I sense that rather than know it. There is no adult I trust, and no adult who loves me unconditionally. I am an object, a toy, a means to an end. When the church tells me God loves me, I have no thoughts about what that could mean or feel like. I have, by sheer force of will, decided to survive my babyhood. I have no concept of God as a loving parent protecting me from harm and delighting in me just because I am. I have never even believed in Santa Claus or the Easter Bunny.

Santa Claus never watches me to see if I am good or bad.

No behavior on my part influences the holiday celebration unless I really dance on someone's last nerve, but that immediately becomes a non-issue when I go into survival mode—Nancy. I am told from the very beginning that Santa Claus is a story and that my dad believes children who believe in Santa Claus will be afraid of the dark. I still have no idea where he got that theory or what made him think that. I sleep with a night light on my entire life. I don't recall being afraid of the dark particularly, although I won't move to an upstairs bedroom for quite a while. My Christmas presents depend on the amount of money available for shopping. My mother makes a show of the Santa Claus story by taking me to see Santa at the department store. No explanation is needed to account for more than one Santa. Every store hires some guy to dress up in the red suit. She reads to me about Santa Claus. I know about the elves, the toy shop at the North Pole, the reindeer—the whole thing. I also know it is a big lie. My parents even take me to Santa Claus, Indiana, one time to look around that happy little place. I don't remember anything about it except there were a lot of really big candy cane painted poles around.

Dad takes a scientific approach on every natural phenomenon. He takes us out on the porch in thunderstorms to watch the lightning and smell the ozone. Nobody in our house ever worries about a storm. We play outside in storms whenever there is no lightning. God isn't mad, bowling or whatever else people tell kids. Storms occur as a result of filled-up clouds, wind and electrical charges built up in the atmosphere. Rainbows can sometimes be seen because sunlight is refracted through water in the air. I am not encouraged to take a romantic view of any natural process. I do read a lot of folk tales, though, so I learn the myths that way.

When it comes to God-theory, I have nothing to go on.

My parents seem to think there is a God, or at least they tell me there is one. Prayer, Dad says, is a thinking process rather than a communication process, where one sorts out one's problems on one's own. No miracles are expected, none occur. We don't pray for guidance, a new bike, an A on a test or a cure. We say grace, but only when company comes. It is fine to read the Bible, and some argument can always be stirred up regardless of who says what. Dad likes sermons on faith, he says. I never remember him praying (other than grace) or reading the Bible. I think he goes to church because Mom wants him to set a good example for us kids. She always sits between me and him because he will play games and distract me from the worship service, and I am nuisance enough by myself. I am allowed to bring a book and read if I want to.

Based on what they tell me at church, I am sure God has no interest in me. I do not expect anything from God either, but I am afraid I am terribly offensive to God. I don't want to be on the outs with God for any reason. I hear that terrible punishment awaits those who get on God's bad side. I can't figure out much I do that would bother the deity that seriously, but I want to be on the safe side. Not having a sense of oneself as a real person, though, does keep one from feeling connected to the universe, however one perceives the universe. I feel connected to nobody and no thing. I'm just here for no apparent reason.

It's safe to hang out at the church. People don't bother me much. I pitch in with whatever projects we are doing—painting a room in the basement for our meetings, making tray favors for the Altenheim, an old folks home, washing cars in the parking lot to make money for projects. I giggle with my girl friends and hold hands with the boys on the school bus we use for occasional outings. I love being around the church because I can be something approaching a normal kid. Everybody is happy to keep up appearances and assume that everything is fine in my home. Now and then, my mother helps out with cooking something, but mostly, my parents stay strictly out of my church life, and I am happy about it. I go to services, often, without them. I love sitting in the big, quiet sanctuary with its oak pews and light green carpet, its stained glass window of Jesus in the garden of Gethsemane, and the cool air almost motionless surrounding me. I can think my own thoughts. I don't have to come up with some plausible response to Mom's intrusive questions. I can be sick or healthy, happy or sad. I am most often sad— depressed, as far as I know, without cause. Mom says I have everything and I have no reason to be sad. She has no patience with what she sees as adolescent moodiness.

At church and at school, I hear a lot about the future. At church, they tell me I need to get my spiritual house in order so I can go to heaven because Jesus has been crucified because I am such a terrible sinner (we all are) that God has had to make this tragic/triumphant statement. At school, I learn that I am responsible for the way the world is going to go in the next twenty years or so, so I'd better stay on track and get myself a good career. The Russians are already in space, and if I don't learn physics there'll be hell to pay on the scientific front. I feel powerless in the face of all this responsibility. I am a good student, but I really don't understand the physical sciences and math as well as the liberal arts. I state that I believe in Jesus Christ as my personal savior while wondering whatever possessed God to think I'm worth that much bother. I am totally at sea, but I am having a pretty good time because I'm out of the house about ten hours a day and then I have four or five hours of homework because I'm in the advanced track at school.

By the time I marry, I am in a complete religious quandary, but no one can guess. I am a counselor at church camp by now, and one day, on a hike, I'm at the back of the group with the current George from my church (we had a string of seminary student pastors named George for several years). "George," I say, "I'm engaged to marry Herb. He wants to go to seminary, but I'm worried."

"Why would you be worried?" George replies.

"Because I have so many doubts about the church and Jesus and all those theological things. Maybe I can't be a minister's wife."

"You'll be fine," he says. "The church needs good, honest doubt."

I think and think about this. Always, at camp, I feel about as close to God as I ever feel. It has to do with being outside so much. They give us a booklet with personal devotions for every day, and each morning before breakfast, we find our own little spot to sit for about ten minutes or so with the booklet and our Bibles. I take this seriously and really try to make some sense out of it all. After breakfast, we have Bible classes, sermons, lectures and activities related to the camp theme until lunch. There are a couple hundred kids at camp, but we are divided into small groups for much of the study. I believe I am about the only person there who has questions or problems with the stuff we're studying. After lunch, there's a quiet time for about forty-five minutes, then we do "campy" stuff like swim, boat, play baseball, hike and so on. Before dinner, we shower and attend to similar personal matters. We sing around the tables for fifteen to thirty minutes at each meal. The evening program is always another kind of activity related to the camp theme. We might see a movie. On one memorable occasion, I am sitting with a girl more naïve than I (if that is believable) and we are watching a film about missionaries in Africa. As it turns out, the African mothers see no reason to diaper their babies, and a naked little boy is shown briefly. The girl next to me screams. She claims to have never seen a naked boy before. "Haven't you ever baby-sat?" I ask. She says she has not.

After the program, we have some form of recreation, then head for the dorms for a Bible study before lights out. The evening ends with the singing of taps from one dorm to another all around the camp. For me, it is heaven on earth. My doubts and fears are accepted, no one teases me about my physical body, my habits or my ideas. I can talk. I can be alone. The camp nurse sees me only if I want to see her. She is not searching me for signs of illness daily. There is so much singing! I love vespers every night beside the lake as the sun is going down. I hate it when camp is over and my parents drive me home.

I have to hand it to the E & R Church on the topics of Bible study and music. We kids are thoroughly grounded in both. Much of the scripture I memorize I learn because I sing it. We begin learning hymns and songs in the nursery department. No babies are left lying around in strange cribs for an hour. We are picked up and sung to. I get to do some of this singing as I get a little older. I take a turn helping in the church nursery every few weeks. I am completely in love with babies.

The Presbyterian Church has much in common with the United Church of Christ, which is what the Evangelical and Reformed Church became after it merged with the Congregational Church in the late '50s. I have no particular problems joining Herb's home church. I think this is important if he's going to seminary—I should be a Presbyterian, too. My dad tells me I won't be going to the same heaven as he is going to. He's teasing, but, actually, that idea is okay by me. I start to worry more and more frequently about the afterlife. The Presbyterians have long since given up the notion of predestination where a person is slated for heaven or hell from birth, and doesn't know until he gets there which one he's assigned to, but eternal fates do exercise the adherents from time to time. My goal in life becomes being a good little pastor's wife, and I succeed admirably.

When my marriage falls apart, Herb says that I am too traditional, which I translate to mean that I'm inhibiting the relationship he's developing with a woman in the congregation he is serving as an interim pastor. She is teaching him transcendental meditation. Neither his mother nor I object to meditation , but we see meditation as a time alone where you study the Bible, pray and rejuvenate yourself for the tasks that otherwise occupy your time. Herb suddenly announces that he's giving up caffeine (he's a notorious addict), and that he has become a follower of some guru. His new girlfriend wants him to drive her to Chicago where the guru is coming for some gathering. She is planning to cook for the guru—her special recipes which do not include roast beef and mashed potatoes. The guru's picture goes up on the dashboard of the family vehicle, and a little shrine to the guru appears in Herb's office. I have no idea what the congregation of the church he is serving thinks about this, but I am pretty sure they aren't going to be supportive.

Now I start getting phone calls from the people in the congregation he previously served and the one he is currently serving. These churches are located in the same area. People are letting me know that the family car has found a new home, as far as they can tell, up at the girlfriend's house which is on a main road. I hear that Herb and the girlfriend are spotted in the health food store in the middle of the day. When I ask Herb about this, he tells me she needs a lot of help because her husband travels and isn't home to deal with the children (they have three) or fix the things that go wrong around a house. My house is practically falling down around me. I have to learn to spackle, paint and hang wallpaper by myself in order to get one child's bedroom habitable. Then I start on the next one. We have moved the kitchen from one large room onto a closed porch which we have had to rebuild, but when our six-year-old's birthday party comes up, I have to lift children over the immense hole in the floor between the two rooms. We have completely remodeled a small barn on the property into a waiting room, office and bath for Herb's business as a pastoral counselor with an open, finished loft on the second floor over the entire area. We have run water and heat out to the barn, repaved the driveway to include a small parking area. I learn to glaze in order to put new glass in the former hayloft door. We turn a staircase one hundred eighty degrees to accommodate clients. I have worked day and night on this project right along with him, but my house is still sporting a twenty-five year old paint job. Just about the time of the divorce, we manage to get the downstairs powder room turned ninety degrees and re-plumbed, but it isn't finished until I am gone.

It's hard to understand why the girlfriend is getting all this assistance. He doesn't even show up at the birthday party I'm giving for our youngest child who is turning six and wants her entire kindergarten class plus some day care friends and her teacher. I try prayer and counseling with a minister friend of ours because Herb says I have a problem. I don't doubt it a bit. I know I'm doing something terribly wrong here, and I am pleading with God to show me what to do. God's advice appears to be "Get out now." At this point, Herb is trying hard to get me to become friends with his girlfriend. He is scheduling picnics, parties and get-togethers. I am not responding very well. I go along with a lot of this stuff to try to protect my interests and my children, but I am distraught beyond belief. Then, Herb tells me I am suffering from a grief reaction because of my mother's sudden death several years previously. I need to grieve and get it over with, he says. So, he sends me and the youngest child off to "Synod School." This is a week-long event held at a Presbyterian college. I have been to Synod School several times, have taught courses there with Herb. It is like a summer camp for families. There are programs for all ages and one of the programs at this particular school (there are a number of Synod Schools all over the country) is on grief management. In five days, some minister from somewhere is going to solve all my problems with my personal death and that of my mother. I'm glad of a chance to get away. The older kids stay at home, and the girlfriend does a lot of babysitting. They go sailing, too. I've never been sailing.

I arrive at Synod School and sign up for the course. For about two hours every morning, a group of about twenty people grapples with life and death. We write up our epitaphs, plan our funerals, talk about afterlife, sing, "Let goods and kindred go, this mortal life also. The body they may kill. God's truth abideth still. His kingdom is forever." This is the last verse of the hymn "A Mighty Fortress Is Our God," a cornerstone Protestant hymn written by Martin Luther, himself. I talk to the instructor outside of class, but I do not feel any different about my mother's death. She is still dead, and I still really don't care much. I am concluding that unexpressed grief is not my problem and neither is concern about the afterlife. My younger daughter is having a great time. She is attending the children's activities where they are trying out all kinds of Sunday School materials and techniques. She is on field trips and outings, making friends and having fun.

As soon as I get home, I am taken to the girlfriend's house so she can give me a foot massage. She is into reflexology and feels competent to diagnose whatever ails me. I am, by now, totally confused. Linnie is on the ascendant with Ted close behind. Nancy is fighting to keep us together socially. Herb continues his crazy behavior. He takes me to an American Psychological Association convention. I hear, and do not register, seminars on child abuse and child development. He tries to learn massage and attends gong meditation. I go with him to one session of gong meditation. I learn that there are an amazing number of sounds to be gotten out of a gong. I am really making an effort to be accepting, cooperative and all that. My in-laws are occasionally dispatching relatives to our house to try to talk sense into Herb.

As winter approaches, Herb comes up with a new plan. Our house is large. It has three floors, two baths and water to the third floor. There are four bedrooms on the second floor and two on the third floor. The family room is not finished (naturally), but there is a big dining room, a large living room and an ample entry hall. The house has a leaded glass door, original paneling, a chandelier, a full basement and there is the finished barn out back plus a small patio. Herb proposes that his girlfriend and her three children move in with us for the winter. She will save a lot of money because she won't have to maintain her house. I will continue working (I now have a public school job to pay for the mansion I'm living in), and she will be the housewife. Since, he says, I do not supervise the children adequately in matters such as homework and after school snacks, she will handle that. My part will be to bring in money as I have the college education (including a masters degree) while she attended a junior college. Her husband will visit at our house when he comes in now and then from California (her home state) where he is now based. He doesn't need to come to Cincinnati much because his business here is finished. She will take over the third floor—but he gets no farther with this scenario before I hit the roof. I tell him he'd better hire a lawyer. He begs me to see Louisville David with him before I "go off the deep end." I never know whether he discussed this idea with his girlfriend or not. I am way beyond caring about that, and my counselor is now telling me that Herb is possibly into an early mid-life crisis (he's forty), but it might last a long time, and I might not want to wait it out. Dern tootin'!

We drive to Louisville. He wants to go to the movies. I don't want to be in the same room with him. We see David who says, "I don't usually advise couples to get a divorce, but you should. Do only what you have to do together—like taxes—but be as if dead to each other." Herb has been arguing that I hate men. David doesn't see this at all. He says I'm merely mad as hell at Herb. This seems accurate to me.

I'm the one who insists that we inform the Presbytery Committee on Ministry that we are divorcing. This is what is supposed to happen, and the chair of the committee at that time is my pastor. I also insist that we tell the other pastor at the church Herb is serving. Herb reluctantly drags himself to these meetings. It is incumbent upon the Presbytery to investigate our proceedings for wrongdoing on his part since, obviously, he cannot serve God appropriately if his own life is not in order. I have banished Herb to the third floor since he refuses to move out of the house. On the night of our eighteenth wedding anniversary, at about 10:30, after I am in bed, a knock comes on my bedroom door. Herb wants to know if I want to go out for ice cream to celebrate. I think not. One day while we are discussing how to divide up our belongings, he suddenly notices that I have taken off my wedding rings. "Oh," he says, "does that mean no more sex?" Duh!

As soon as I can make arrangements, I buy a small house not too far away. I don't want to take the kids out of their school. I am minding my own business when the phone rings one evening. It is Herb and he wants to know if I will tell the Session of his current church that his girlfriend, who is almost a live-in at this time, is not the reason for our divorce. I say I'm not going to lie. In due course, someone from the Session calls me for my version of the story. I don't lie. Then I have to have a couple of glasses of wine.

The children have trouble at school over the whole miserable mess. An article about Herb and the guru (this guy hasn't left yet) appears in the newspaper, and they are questioned, teased and generally harassed by the other kids. One child goes to a youth group overnight and another kid points out to her that what her father is doing is adultery. Jesus has come out quite strongly against adultery, so her father will be going straight to Hell. Just thought she should know. She comes home and asks me about this. What should I tell her? Girlfriend gets her divorce right away, too, and Herb remarries about four months after our divorce is final. It would have been sooner, but they had to wait on her husband to get to town.

Herb and his wife are good to the children. I never have any trouble about child support, and they help fund camps, outings, clothes and so on. They attend performances at the school, take the kids on vacation and offer their home (my old place) for parties. Herb and I have agreed, for the sake of the children, that we will be cordial to one another, that we will not deprive them of a parent. I think both of us did well in not abusing the other to the children. My policy is to let the children make their own judgments about their dad. We cooperate on gift-giving so that the children receive what they would have received had we stayed married. We give one confirmation party, one graduation party, one wedding shower and one baby shower, as the occasion demands. Karen's friends can hardly believe that, not only can her dad and I sit in the kitchen and have friendly conversation while they celebrate their high school graduation in the dining room, but Karen and I had had Thanksgiving Dinner with him and his wife. Sometimes that's the best way to handle things.

I have yet to remember my childhood, so I blame all problems—physical, mental, spiritual—on the divorce. Most people seem to agree that I am the wronged party. They just can't get over Herb's behavior. He leaves the church he's serving, is given to know he's unwelcome in the one I attend, which he served previously, and he flounders for a while until the Presbytery agrees that he can serve as a "Stated Supply" to a small church in a neighboring community. A Stated Supply is not the same as an installed pastor. His salary is determined by the Presbytery rather than the church. The church is usually in decline for some reason, and unable to afford an installed pastor. They pay what they can, and the Stated Supply is generally a part-time position. The first church he has in this capacity is one where a minister made a full career. When the man retired, it took the congregation a long time to get back on its feet, review its priorities and get in a position to hire an installed pastor again. The second church was near death after a series of interim pastors.

Night Terror

Shaking, quaking, waiting to throw up,
Scared of that looming figure so big in the night.

Night comes in daylight,
Even with candy and books to read.
Terror strikes, hurts me, shocks me,
Takes away my goodness,
Leaves me afraid of everybody.

Nine

Almost unencumbered. I have only three children, a dog and a parakeet to worry about. I have no job, and it is summer, so I can't get a teaching job right away. The day I am fired for "conflict of interest," I go into shock for a while. I took the job when a "reduction in force" found me low man on the seniority totem pole. The place I'm fired from doesn't want to pay unemployment for me, so we end up in a hearing with a referee. A lawyer I'm dating goes with me, which is good because I come out of the hearing with unemployment benefits. Friends have started to send over bags of groceries, but child support and alimony keep body and soul together. Herb never shirks in that department. He never gives me extra money, but always the right amount at the right time, and I am grateful for that.

By fall, I've discovered the student loan. I get one, and go back to school to certify to teach learning-disabled and behavior-disordered children. I need twelve hours, which are offered after school hours and on Saturdays, so I am able to substitute-teach during the week. This reduces my unemployment benefit, but brings me enough money with the loan to manage. I'm lucky enough to get one long-term assignment for about six weeks while someone recovers from surgery, and I pick up a couple of students as a homebound instructor. The rest of the time, I get calls on a daily basis. I sub in French, German and Spanish classes because I have a minor in French from undergraduate days. I teach shop and driver's ed (classroom only). I get to be a fairly familiar face at this big high school where years before, I had interned with the school counselor. I am all over the high school and the junior high, but I'm not certified for elementary school, so they can't use me there. They don't want to hire me, though.

Just as I am about to give up on finding a new job, I hear about an opening in the same bunch that let me go in the "rif" situation. I interview and get the job. I am overjoyed, and, because I'll be a special education teacher, I will not have to repay the student loan if I teach for five years. It doesn't look like I'll ever be able to stop teaching. I have all these kids and animals plus myself to feed, clothe and house. I'm looking at a teacher's salary, but it is a lot more than the salary I was fired from, and the benefits are marvelous. In the job arena, I am nervous, but happy.

Due to all this job crisis, I am letting my social life deteriorate. I can't afford to hang around with my neighborhood friends because we are living in a wealthy suburban area. I don't mind spending time alone, but the kids are still in trauma from the divorce. Most of our social life has been family oriented, and we have especially spent time with two families in particular. This all changes because I am divorced. It's not that these people are not friends with me anymore, but it is awkward to include an "odd" duck in the parties, picnics and get-togethers. Some of these folks still have to deal with Herb in various ways; some of them are the ones who have kept me posted on his extracurricular activities and some just can't believe that a minister and his wife can have problems. Also, I am working full-time while my friends stay at home, meet for coffee, shop together or volunteer at school. I'm not knocking these lifestyles, but it's not a way I can afford to be any more. I feel that I'm doing good work—important work—and I feel professional for the first time in my life. I glimpse an adult for a change.

Inside, I envy my friends, though. I am working, at this point, out of necessity rather than choice. Also, they have loving husbands. Their marriages aren't perfect, but they are willing to put forth effort (as are their husbands) to keep their marriages functioning well. Our worlds now are in different galaxies. I start to think that if I had a husband, my life would be better. I could rejoin the community. I envision a wonderful man with a steady job who loves my children like I do. This, of course, is sheer fantasyland drivel, but a person needs goals, right? The search is on.

My nephew has married a beautiful young woman he met through a dating service. His experience has been good, so why shouldn't auntie try it? No good reason—until I actually meet the men the service recommends. My first mistake is to prefer a non-smoker and moderate drinker. The next error is specifying someone with a Christian outlook. One disaster after another occurs. One date never even makes it through a cup of coffee. One guy wants me to come to his place and cook. Another one is so full of himself and his stock car racing that he doesn't even inquire about what I do for a living, but he does want to know how tall I am. Yet another tries to impress me with his knowledge of how to set up microphones for a Christian rock concert to be held in his church. We are meeting at his favorite church buddies' hang out. I see instantly that these are not my kind of Christian people. I'm singing Mozart, Schubert and Haydn for religious kicks.

Friends fix me up with noted losers of all ages. I realize I'm a loser and disappointment to them, too. I'm getting nowhere fast. Next I try a singles' fellowship at a nearby church. This is one of the largest groups in the country, and every Sunday evening, several hundred singles turn up for a staggering array of activities. I am reluctant to give up "Sixty Minutes," and "inadequately" supervising my children, but I go anyway. I do not get caught up in the magic. All my alter personalities are well underground as far as I know. Nancy is in full operation. Since Nancy has no feelings, I do not relate to people very well and find it hard to get acquainted with any of them. I am persuaded by a single friend to go to a New Year's Eve party that the group is sponsoring, mostly because it is in the neighborhood.

Marcia and I arrive at the appointed hour. No good. One should come late to these affairs because it then appears that one's social calendar is so full that one has only just had a moment to drop by and greet one's little crowd at the singles' party. We are on time. Hardly anyone is there. We pick out a spot and park ourselves in it. We will have a good time if it kills us and several innocent bystanders. When we get ourselves situated with a soft drink for me and wine for her plus a bowl of chips, some men and women of our casual acquaintance fill in spots at the table. The place is starting to get crowded, and we are pleased. We might meet men. The dancing starts, and, sure enough, I get an invitation to dance.

I've never met H before. He's reasonably handsome, well-groomed and looks very nicely turned out in his dark suit. Some very strange chord tugs when he touches me. I don't recognize it, but it seems kind of comfortable and exciting at the same time. We dance together most of the evening, and when we aren't dancing, we are talking. It's like being fifteen again. Even though I'm forty-something, I have braces on my teeth. My parents didn't think my crooked, crowded teeth needed fixing, so I had to suffer the embarrassment of buck teeth and a receding chin until I could afford to pay for my own orthodontia. This metal mouth doesn't seem to bother H in the least. He's saying I'm something special. I think he must be getting his information from the mother ship, but it sure is fun to think I'm fascinating, a brilliant conversationalist and amazingly, attractive.

The courtship is on! The clinching argument for accepting that first date to the race track is the fact that H wants to bring along an elderly man whom he has befriended. The old man loves the races. Would I come to the racetrack, too? He plays the oldies on the radio—"When Swing Was King" is the name of the show. He drives a car about ten years old but loaded with every electronic gadget. When he takes my hand to escort me to the grandstand, I get a rush that startles me. I briefly think, "Dad."

After the races, we drop off his friend and go to the Art Museum. It is free on Saturdays. We wander around through the exhibits until closing. He doesn't want to leave me, apparently, so I call home to be sure the children are okay, and we go off, ostensibly, to see a movie. When we arrive at the theater, we are late, or something. At any rate, we do not see the picture. H is so smitten that he wants to park somewhere. We find a spot, and contrary to everything I've ever believed or tried to live by, we make love in that big old car. Unfortunately, the car is now stuck in mud. No amount of gunning the motor is helping. We have to pick our way out of a field, walk to a house, and convince the owner that we are not serial killers, but people who need a tow truck. I call home again, feeling very foolish. I tell the children the car is in the mud, and they say, "Oh, yeah?"

The first parking incident leads to many other similar incidents, only we give up the car as housing. We manage to get ourselves alone at my house all the time. H. rarely even sees my children, but I am stubbornly set on the idea that he and the kids will just love each other. I am feeling guilty now about how much sex we have. I think I'm neglecting my family, and I know I am lying to them—not that they are unaware of it. We never go to H's place because he is still living with his parents. This should have been a red flag, but I am blissfully ignorant of the color red at this time. If friends try to tell me I am headed for disaster, I don't listen or even register their comments or questions. I want to know everything about H. After a while, he is forthcoming. Again, I should have seen trouble lurking. I am snookered in by the resemblance to my old relationship with Dad. H even looks a little like him.

Early on in the relationship, I learn about the eccentricities of my new love's family. I am sworn to secrecy in a complex system of duping their friends and relatives. The deal is that they own three houses, all in Cincinnati, and live in two of them. This doesn't strike me as particularly odd until I find out how it all works. I'll call them houses A, B and C. House A is where they live during the week. It is a house where they have lived for many years, a lot of them with the original owner, H's grandmother. This house is never seen by anybody outside the family, although the neighbors are known. Neighbors are visited outside on the porch, if at all. House B is the "official" residence. It is the house where guests are entertained. The family treks there on weekends. House A is not to be seen, but one evening, H takes me there when his parents are out of town. There is "stuff" to the ceiling in every room, and narrow pathways through the rooms. Newspapers and magazines are piled neatly around two or three rooms. The kitchen is loaded with odds and ends of bottles, dishes, glassware, packaged food, silverware, linens, tables, chairs to the point where I can't tell what kind of flooring is in place. Furniture crowds every room. Clothes hang on doors, books tumble out of bookshelves. The light is dim. H explains that his mother is going through all this stuff that she's inherited from relatives, and will soon have it all sorted out. This never happens during my history with this bunch. There are people who do not know this house even exists, and there are others who do not know House B exists. I am to keep these people straight and not mention the fact that there are two addresses for the same family. If one of the homes was in Palm Beach, maybe. These houses are about twenty minutes apart.

House B is typical suburbia. It is a little over-furnished, but quite nice. It has some beautiful antiques and is reasonably neat and clean. I am allowed in this house almost any weekend for a visit. I can go in all the rooms, unlike House A where it was not safe to climb the stairs. I am never to let on that I even know about House A, even though the family talks about it. I don't know what I'm supposed to think about this. There is a lovely yard with House B, flower gardens and a large patio. We celebrate everything at this house. There is a ritual for every celebration, and there is never anyone but the family invited, unless, like me, one is now engaged to be married to the son of the family. The ritual does not vary from year to year. Birthdays are dinner at a restaurant (H's mother cooks only on Christmas Day because everything is closed), then birthday cake, ice cream and certain birthday songs back at the house. On non-celebration days, after dinner out, there is usually a little drive around to look at houses in nearby areas, and to comment on the architecture, decoration and yard maintenance. Some of these places are visited frequently enough that changes in progress can be observed. Then, it's back to the house to visit, and, possibly, watch something on TV. The programs are carefully monitored for potential unpleasant topics such as religion, politics or suggestive content. We watch only "safe" shows. I am usually asked something about "your dear mother" and I have to pretend she was the lovely person everyone expects her to have been. Fortunately, my dad rarely comes up. They really like to talk about their relatives better. At some fairly early hour, I am driven home, and H rushes back to whichever house they're sleeping at tonight. He carries an overnight bag in the trunk of his car. He does not keep things like shaving gear, pajamas and what have you at House B.

House C is empty. They do not wish to rent it or sell it. They prefer to do whatever maintenance is required and pay the taxes on it. I am not really supposed to know about this house either, but H takes me there. One idea is that much of the stuff from House A will be stored, ultimately, in House C, and sold from there. This doesn't happen during my watch. In fact, years later, I have occasion to pass this house on my way to chorus rehearsal, and it appears empty still. As soon as H and I are married, I suggest to him that we buy that house from his parents and restore it as it is beautiful and in a nice, if busy, area of the city. My children are getting older and won't be too upset by a move, I think, but I'm probably wrong. Anyway, his parents will not sell it to us. Someday, those three houses will be his problem. I'm so thankful they won't be mine!

H and I marry almost a year to the day from when we

meet. It is a nice party, but I nearly have to drag Karen down the aisle. She doesn't want this to happen, and she is the most honest person present. Everybody else is coddling me along in my crazy euphoria about how great life is now going to be. She is calling it like she sees it—and she's only about eleven years old—but she is absolutely right. I was invited to Herb's second wedding, but I don't invite him to mine.

Once I'm married again, things start going downhill. H complains about the children. They are not sufficiently respectful, they do not like his parents, they are demanding and selfish. They, on the other hand, resent him for being there at all and for trying to tell them what to do, for demanding obedience to him and for begrudging them any little thing. He keeps a mental record of the times he drives them someplace or runs some errand for me, and he expects some kind of compensation. He acts like a guest in the house. He doesn't want to help with any chores, refuses to clear the table one night when I'm sick, goes to cut grass at his parents' place, but reluctantly cuts ours. He cannot keep a job. He is educated as a teacher, but has no ability in the classroom, so he takes sales jobs. He is extremely gullible and falls for any sales pitch that comes at him. He actually believes commercials. In the four years we are married, he has fifteen jobs—no lie. He pays me "rent" toward household expenses, but seldom has money for anything like car repairs to any vehicle but his own. He pays for his own clothes, and he is fairly generous with me as far as entertainment and gifts go. He cannot cook anything, nor does he clean up anything. About all he does is cut the grass. While he is unemployed, I ask him to paint the bathroom. Doesn't happen.

The very first crisis in this marriage occurs about four months into it. I have become pregnant, apparently on the honeymoon—two miserable days in Louisville touring Churchill Downs. Though we have not taken many precautions to prevent this from happening, I haven't worried much because I think I have just about reached menopause. I am in my early forties—too late. I think. Besides, I have not had an easy time of becoming pregnant with the other three children. I think the symptoms are menopause until a friend suggests otherwise. I seek out the doctor. "You're pregnant," he says. "I won't do an abortion, but I can give you the name of somebody who will."

I look at him, totally amazed. He has made a major assumption here. "I haven't asked for an abortion," I said. "I want to talk this over with my family."

We talk about the situation. H is incredulous. "I did that?" he asks.

"You, and none other," I reply. "What do you want to do?"

"I come down on the side of life."

"Okay."

I have to get some maternity clothes right away because I'm moving into the fourth month, I'm older, my muscles are slack and I'm already showing. I start thinking how this new baby is going to work out with everything else I'm doing. I have maintained my involvement with the church (I'm now an Elder serving on Session, singing in the choir, helping with Christian Education and miscellaneous other activities). I'm working full-time, and I don't know what I'll actually do with a baby. Day care? Sitter at home? I can't stay home myself—we'll all starve. The doctor insists on a bunch of tests since I am so old and it has been so long since my last baby. He starts out with ultrasound, and it's exciting to see a tiny person floating around inside me even, though it looks like a blob to me.

Although this is H's family's first and last chance at immortality, they do not want to see the ultrasound picture of their grandchild. This is because it proves we've been having sex, and they consider the picture just as obscene as a picture of me naked. It startles them considerably to know that my son, who is taking classes at Cincinnati Art Institute, is not only drawing naked people on a daily basis, but he actually knows some of the models. Jeff says it's easier to draw people he knows. To me, that's strange. They certainly know my relationship with their son is not platonic, and they know where babies come from. Perhaps they are just not getting up their hopes after all these years

Now the doctor orders amniocentesis to check for Down's Syndrome or other genetic problems that occur often in older pregnant women. I drag H in with me for the procedure. It is not a really big deal, but I can see that he isn't going to hold up well under medical conditions. What if the baby or I get sick? He won't have any idea what to do. I see I'm going to have to rely on my doctor and my friends.

One Saturday morning, we have an appointment with the doctor to go over the results of the testing. It has taken a couple of extra weeks to get this information even though the tests are all handled locally. I am scared because I believe the baby has stopped moving. I don't have a good feeling about the interview. It is good that I feel that way because all the news is bad news. The baby is a girl. She has a genetic disorder called Turner Syndrome, which is not too terrible in and of itself, although it is certainly no walk in the park. People with Turner Syndrome may have an assortment of problems, but the main one is that they do not have gonads, so they are sterile and do not go through puberty without hormone therapy. If this is the only problem, I think we can handle it, but that's not all. Our little girl has the worse case of spina bifida anybody around here has ever seen. The reason the test results were so long in coming back is that the hospital here sent them on to the Mayo Clinic because they couldn't believe the alpha fetal protein level. It went off the chart. The baby will never do any of the physical things babies do since her spine is almost completely open. So, the doctor says she will not live, she can't live. Do I want to go ahead with the abortion he is now willingly recommending, or do I want to wait and let nature take its course? There could be other problems, too. He has discussed this with his partner in practice as well as other professionals. Every one agrees that this baby doesn't have a chance.

H wants to think about it. We should go home and come back on Monday for a further check-up and a decision.

It's a sad weekend at my house. The children have been getting excited about having a baby brother or sister. I actually cry about this, which is out of character for me. Nancy doesn't cry about anything, but this gives me an occasion to regret a lot of things, not just the baby. I am realizing my folly at having married the second time, but I am ashamed to admit it. My life is clearly not working out in any way, shape or form as I intended. While in many ways it is a blessing to be able to skip the trouble and expense of another child, still it is our child. I would possibly have considered abortion early on, but I didn't know I was pregnant until the embryo stage was passed. I am uncomfortable with abortions after the first trimester. I am totally convinced, however, that this baby has died anyway. It is a moot point to ponder whether I am up to the challenge of a disabled child.

On Monday, we report to the doctor's office. He agrees with me that probably the baby has died. I don't think he believes that I felt her move earlier, but I know that feeling and it's gone. He sends me on to the hospital from his office. My husband stays with me while the nurses start IV medications to lessen nausea. My doctor shows up with an intern who's learning to do this procedure. The intern is going to do the honors until it is time to deliver the baby. I receive prostaglandins to start labor. In short order, I'm as sick as I can be. H is useless. He sits in a chair all day and periodically says he's sorry I have to go through this. Of course, there's really not much he can do. The baby has to come out of my body. Finally, late that night, the doctor determines that it's time to deliver. Do I want to be awake or asleep? I choose asleep. I've had enough. May he autopsy the baby? Yes. We want to know the full extent of the problems. Does H want to be there for the birth? Emphatically, no.

I miss a week of school. I feel fine afterward, and am glad it's over. The doctor has already told me that the baby was stillborn, had been dead for several days, he thought. My friends send over prepared meals. H's parents send some uncooked food. They express no concern directly to me, but H brings word that they are glad I'm all right. A couple of weeks later, when we are visiting his parents, no one mentions the whole baby thing except for my father-in-law who grabs a moment when his wife is out of the room to say, "I'm sorry for your loss."

When I go back to the doctor for the check-up, he gives me the autopsy report. Not only does the baby have the Turner Syndrome and the spina bifida, but she has an extra heart chamber, and one of her ureters is not even connected to her kidney. I know I've done the right thing, that, in fact, nature would have done the right thing for me, but there would have been risk to me in the process.

I soldier on in the marriage for almost three more years. I realize that this is not going anywhere. I am not enjoying my life. I feel that I've got a fourth child just as surely as if I'd actually given birth. H tells me that if we should divorce, he would go right back to live with his parents, and "follow their rules." He doesn't want to follow my rules, he says, because I am not his mother. I am on the Session at my church by now, and sometimes, the meetings run late. He comes up to the church when he thinks it's time for the meeting to be over and hangs around to be sure I'm okay. We live in the safest neighborhood in Cincinnati. He doesn't like it if I talk to the pastor in the meeting room as people are leaving. He attends church with me. Despite having a very fine voice, he doesn't want to sing in the choir with me. He doesn't want to do much of anything except go out to dinner and go bar-hopping with a friend of his now and then when the friend comes back to town to visit relatives. H wants to be a single man living at home. I want my pre-marriage life back.

I have tried normality and found it seriously wanting. I have learned something about who I am—a weird person. I haven't yet met any of my alters, but I know I am not a typical person. I am becoming more alienated from everything and everybody. I want to run away again, but now I own the house, so that would be difficult. I take the next best step. I tell H to leave. It's over. He is not particularly perturbed by this. We don't argue or wrangle over belongings. I am paying all the bills anyway, and he doesn't owe me money, but I have had to go into debt because of some of his problems. At this point, I say, "Never mind. Just go." We even use the same lawyer to save money on our dissolution. I return to my birth name, which makes the third name change for my family and friends to get used to. The children use their father's name all along.

Pecking Out

Cramped inside the shell,
Bent at every joint,
Ovoid, wet, sticky, stiff,
A naked little bird has had enough.
Sunlight winks into the first tiny hole.
The chick pecks on,
A hundred days of pecking. ...
At last, a crack, a split!
Light pours in blinding.
Flying can wait.
Pecking out's enough for now.

Ten

My son, through all this time, has some serious problems. His adolescence holds plenty of terrors for me. I worry a great deal about his safety and health. I can put up with the unorthodox hairstyles and the thrift shop chic, but some of his behaviors really scare me. His drug use and unauthorized trips out of town are a major part of my emotional unbalance at this time. I am certain that all of his problems are directly my fault because I'm a terrible mother and have failed my beautiful son. I manage to keep him at home through high school. He attends his graduation ceremony, saying, "I'm only doing this for you, Mom." He has proven himself to be a fine artist. He wins, in spite of it all, a scholarship to an art school in Savannah, Georgia. He wants to go to San Francisco Art Institute. I have a good long battle with myself not to go crazy here.

Every fiber of my being wants Jeff to go to some nice university right around here, and become some middle class professional person. But, see, he's really my son. He's weird like me. He is the child most like me in outlook and temperament. We share a number of interests, and he has a sense of humor compatible with mine. I am not about to throw him to the wolves in California, but he is set on going. The San Francisco Art Institute likes his portfolio and agrees to match his scholarship, which is renewable. I understand his need to get out of the stifling Midwest and to be his own person. I am not willing to let him go by himself.

In an unprecedented move, I decide to drive him to San Francisco myself and help him get enrolled and settled. I have never driven more than about five hundred miles in any direction before. We get hold of a car somebody wants delivered to Marin County and load up Jeff's worldly possessions. There really aren't that many since a flood in our house five years before wiped out most of his stuff. We agree on how we are going to do this. He wants to camp out along the way, but I want to save some time by staying in motels. If we camp, we'll have to stop early enough to set up our tent. Both of us are experienced campers. He went on his first camping trip at the age of six weeks. The minister's family can rarely afford to vacation any other way, and my dad had once built a boat in our backyard, so my birth family camped for years, boating into campsites.

We decide we will stay in motels but picnic most of our meals. We will change drivers as needed and the passenger gets to be DJ. The DJ gets to select the music. We hear Mozart, John Rutter, Pink Floyd and a full range of other rock and roll greats. The trip is fun. We see every state capital between Ohio and California. We do not stop at the casinos in Nevada because neither one of us is interested in gambling. When we arrive in San Francisco, we spend a little time at Fisherman's Wharf, but Jeff is anxious to get on with his life. We have made arrangements to stay with Herb's sister who lives just north of San Francisco. We cross the

Golden Gate Bridge for the first time, and arrive in good order. That very first night we deliver the car and catch a bus back to Judy's house.

I am thrilled with my independence as much as Jeff is thrilled with his. We have just done something incredible. We've come about 2,600 miles on our own. I am doing the parent things that need to be done without help. When I leave to fly back home, it breaks my heart to leave my "baby," even though he is still staying with his aunt while trying to find an apartment. I know that Judy will see to it that he is settled before school starts. He has a couple of months to do it in. I have jet lag, grief and an imminent move myself to deal with.

Now I'm down to one child at home. Karen is starting high school. The house is getting to be too much to handle financially and physically. There is a lot of upkeep with any house, and, although my children laugh when I buy my own tool box, they stop when I replace two window panes and some heat ducts, including installing something called a thimble between the furnace and the outside of the house. This requires a small batch of concrete to set the piece in place. Previously, the only thimble I'd known anything about went on the finger you used to push a needle through fabric. When I change the leaky faucets on the bathtub, I do need to ask Herb to come over and tighten them. I joke that I need brawn, not brains, for the job. I also call on the husbands of a couple of friends for a few chores where I didn't have the right tools. One of them, Mick, gives me channel locks for Christmas—my own set! I am thrilled. My brother even expresses amazement when I take the trap off one of his sinks to find a contact lens that has gone down the drain. It's not that I can't handle the upkeep, but I don't want to anymore.

I'm tired of cutting the grass, putting up storm windows, fixing this little thing and that little thing. I don't want to paint anything. I had Jeff climb up on the roof on his graduation day to put some screening over the chimney. I am also tired of birds falling into the fireplace.

About a week after I get back from California, I am moving out of my house and into the apartment on Springfield Pike. There is not a great lifestyle change happening here because we've only moved about a mile or so down the street. I am reasonably happy, though my divorce from H is taking a long time to finalize. Karen and I start our respective schools, and I think life is about to become livable again.

My job, teaching emotionally disturbed children, is stressful. Many of my students are survivors of child abuse, and some of them continue to live in less than optimum circumstances. I have a connection to them, but I don't know why. I think that part of my depression must be related to what I think is my compassion for these children. Since I don't recognize my own abuse yet, I believe I'm just a another caring teacher—there are a lot of them—who wants to contribute to society by educating the young people. All thoughts of high school or college teaching have left me. I am teaching eight- to ten-year-olds, but I feel called to do this. In spite of my rationalizations about my work, I still can't shake the blues. I feel worthless, sad, don't sleep too well and constantly cave in to Karen no matter what she wants. I have to rely on Herb and Laura to keep me from just turning Karen loose. I am tired of making decisions and not sure that I can do it anyway. I overlook all accomplishments.

Laura now announces she wants to marry her boyfriend. We all like him, and if this is what she wants, no one is going to stand in her way. I have now started therapy, but the full force of what I've experienced hasn't hit yet. I worry about Laura's marriage and whether or not she's been abused herself. I don't think so, but I have to wonder. I look over her potential in-laws carefully. They seem like nice, normal people with the usual assortment of problems and successes. Herb likes them. I start making Laura's wedding gown, two of three bridesmaids' dresses, and a flower girl dress for her fiance's niece who is also his goddaughter. Laura will be married in a Catholic ceremony, but because she is a Presbyterian, there are some hoops to jump through. I have to help her out a little.

Meanwhile, I've acquired Cleo and my younger daughter is dissatisfied with our living arrangements. I never know just what it is that Karen doesn't like, but she complains about the landlady. Probably this is just teenage rebellion and angst, but I am ill-equipped to deal with it. We move again, and, this time, we go from the frying pan into the fire. First of all, we have to give Herb's address as Karen's official address since the new apartment is outside the city limits of Wyoming, the city we have lived in all along. In Ohio, there are many incorporated villages and cities within a county, so some communities, like Norwood, are independent of the city of Cincinnati, yet completely surrounded by it. It is a complicated system. Now I live in Cincinnati, but Herb lives in the city of Wyoming, about a mile and a half away. I call the school. I say he and I share custody of Karen, which is a little fib, although she is free to see him at any time. We have no particular schedule for that. The school people say she can legally attend Wyoming or Cincinnati Public Schools. I choose not to take her out of Wyoming Schools where she has been her entire life.

The school issue is the least of our worries. The neighbor

in the new place begins complaining and harassing the day we move in. He is unhappy that we prop the outside door open while we move furniture up a flight of stairs. The fact that about six of us are in and out of the door for a couple of hours does not affect his sense that we are letting in thugs, hoodlums, murderers and gang rapists to have the run of the place. He also gripes that we do not finish until a few minutes after 10:00 at night, and comes upstairs to tell us that we have to stop what we're doing because it's now "quiet time." Nobody, including the rental agent, mentioned a "quiet time," so I have to wonder about that. Later on, he complains about my playing Mozart on the piano, the dog barking occasionally and the size of the dog.

Things go along uneasily for a few months. The other neighbors are delightful, no problems there. I take around a letter to them which they will sign if the dog is not bothering them. They all cheerfully sign, and regale me with tales of their unfortunate encounters with our mutual neighbor. I am getting into some deep issues in therapy and my neighbor is no help because I am realizing for the first time what a difficult time I have relating to men who are at all authoritarian.

I am finding out that I cannot deal with a man who gets angry and shouts. I stay away from men as much as I can. Linnie is peeking out from behind the rock and is not seeing much that is different from what she went back there to escape in the first place. Ted has gone underground. Nancy is doing her best to keep things together. Tank Girl is checking the guns. I finally tell the neighbor that if he ever comes to my door again, I will call the police. I have to sit down after that and recover. I am in the midst of remembering how Dad yelled and stomped around, how angry he got and how afraid I was that he'd turn his wrath on me. I don't remember his ever hitting me, but I am terrorized all the same. People who are in some kind of authority over me scare me. I stay away from them. I am not forthcoming to my boss, for instance, when there is any incident. I live in an agony over my lesson plans because they might not suit the boss. Information is constantly streaming from a large number of sources about how to teach, and what to do to improve classroom management. New ideas are popping like popcorn, and it seems to me that I am supposed to implement each and every one or lose my job. I am annually petrified by the writing of individual education plans for my students. In these, I have to document the problems the student is having, but I cannot recommend "parent-ectomy" as a solution, even though in some cases, it would be the solution. I wonder what my own teachers thought about me, wonder if a parent-ectomy would have done me any good. I start to regret what I could have been, and disregard what I am.

Every day, I am beleaguered by children whose language would make a sailor blush, who have no appreciation for education at all, who are mad at me for insisting that they stay in my classroom. I won't let them watch TV all day, wander around the room playing with whatever they find, talk back to adults or eat except at lunch time. If they do not complete their work, they don't get to go out for recess. I ignore their name-calling, but lower their daily ratings when they call me "fuckin' bitch," "asshole," and—my personal favorite—"black bastard." These kids have no idea what they are saying, but they know that their words can get adults mad. I struggle not to take it personally, but it is difficult to be bombarded all day with this stuff, and more, to be told directly that what you are doing is not wanted. I have had students who were thrilled when they learned something, but seldom grateful to the teacher who taught it to them. I know that without my assistant, I will not last in this classroom longer than ten minutes.

Of course, funds are limited. Most of all, the measures we can use to discipline the children are highly limited. Furthermore, we have them only about six hours a day. The other eighteen, they are observing no type of rules, control or discipline in the majority of cases. When I get out a balance scale for a math lesson, one student says he knows what that is because his mother uses a scale like that to weigh drugs. There is really nothing I can do about that. I check. I call the Department of Human Services, the child protection people. Mostly they already know these families and are trying to work with them, but they don't have money either. There is insufficient mental health care in our community, and the parents of our students are unreliable when it comes to keeping appointments, giving medications and, in general, cleaning up their act. There are exceptions, of course, and these students really benefit from what we are doing. They become our "success stories." I am now starting to see myself in some of my students. I learn to know their alters where they exist. One student has an alter personality who can do math. I try to draw out that part of him every day at math time, and it works. One kid has an invisible friend. I speak to the invisible kid as necessary, encouraging him to sit with my student and help him with his work. Not every teacher is willing to do this sort of thing, but I know that it's important.

My personal therapy is hectic now. I am impatient, and want to get this matter settled once and for all. It's too bad that life doesn't work that way. I am fighting on all fronts. Therapist David is not really capable, in my opinion, of addressing all the problems, especially the physical and spiritual ones. Not being a woman is a distinct disadvantage for him here, so I get involved with a group called VOICES in Action, although I think it was simply VOICES at that time. The word VOICES stands for Victims of Incest Can Emerge Survivors. Right from the start, the emphasis is on thriving, not merely surviving.

VOICES has some odd (to me) rules and practices, but, in retrospect, they make a lot of sense. For instance, we meet in a small discussion group. I never see more than about ten women at a meeting. Like AA, we use first names or fictitious names as we choose. For weeks I don't acknowledge that the leader of my small group is a woman I have known for years. She was a member of one of Herb's churches, and quite active in it. In the group, we are not encouraged to become friends with one another. There should be no going out for coffee after meetings or Saturday movie get-togethers or anything of the sort. Once or twice in the three or four years I am active, someone gives a party or picnic and invites the rest of us, but even these are not well attended. People in that much pain and distrust aren't taking any more chances on getting hurt. Most of the time, I have no idea who the others are beyond "Barbara" or "Marie" or whatever. Once we leave the group, we are free to pursue friendships if we want, of course, but I have lost track of all but one or two of my companions on this peculiar journey.

We are a strange bunch that assembles once a week to encounter our personal and group miseries and fears. We are from every walk of life, various ages, assorted educational levels, usually the same race, although that's no barrier. Some of us look like hell, but we've all been there and have the mental "souvenirs" to prove it. A couple of women bring stuffed toys or dolls to hug while we meet. The tissue box is always full. We might have water or another drink with us, but this is no social hour. We are all business, complete with newsprint easel and markers.

First on the agenda, is a "check-in." We go around the circle, each woman describing, briefly, how she is feeling as the group begins. I normally say "pass." I don't know how I feel besides numb, confused or mad, and even if I had a clue, I wouldn't share it. I can't trust anybody with my feelings. They've been discounted so much I don't even recognize feelings in other people well. This is acceptable to the group—they are, if not in the same condition, only a hairsbreadth beyond it. Some start crying right then and there. Others, like me, are stoic. I fancy myself above all this nonsense of feelings. I want to intellectualize the whole business and keep Nancy from dominating the scene yet again.

Next, we do a little relaxation exercise. For a long time, I don't join in. I am afraid to relax because I have kept my guard up for over forty years. I have no idea how to relax, and even if I did, I wouldn't because I don't trust these women as far as I could throw them. I usually leave the room when the relaxing starts and hope that somebody remembers to call me when they're done. Being able to relax never comes easily to me, but I improve. Finally, after a year or so, I can at least close my eyes and stay in the room.

The main work of the evening follows. We must first determine a topic to discuss. While it is fine to bring up any topic, everyone has to agree to talk about it. We are told to veto any and every suggestion if we are uncomfortable with it. One person can say no and the topic is dropped. Some nights it takes some doing. We do not negotiate whether or why or how we will discuss a topic. It is either acceptable to everyone or not. No reasons need be given. The process is not time-limited, per se, but we try to reach consensus quickly.

Topic selected, the person who suggests it usually speaks first. She says whatever she wants to say about it. No interruptions are allowed. She speaks her piece. No one gives her advice, commiserates with her, yells "Right on!" or in any way interacts with her. Occasionally the leader or someone may ask for clarification of some point. We listen respectfully to whatever the speaker says. When she is finished, another person talks on the subject. There may be nods or encouraging smiles, but that's it. No judgments are passed, no comments made. Each woman has an opportunity to speak on the topic. This no-comment stuff drives me up the wall. I have plenty of experience and advice about almost any topic, and I want to babble it right out, but the rules are the rules. Gradually, I come to realize that this is not like the usual therapy group. I don't want any advice. I just want to be heard for once in my life. I want to be respected just as a human being. Since we know very little about each other and have all agreed to a confidentiality policy, it is exciting to say whatever I want to say. Nobody is going to give putdowns or make nice or discount what I say. If I'm lying, it's my problem, but it isn't tempting to lie. When nobody is commenting at all, there's no need to lie to look smarter or cleverer or more confident. We are all so smashed down and warped by what our perpetrators did, we see no value in lying or denying. We're there to get to truth, and, if not justice, at least some kind of personal peace.

Despite the safe atmosphere, I take, literally, months to speak up at all. I eventually figure out that since my memories are preverbal, I don't know any words to say. Babies remember everything, but they do it in terms of feelings, not words. I have flashbacks all the time. I smell a certain aftershave and suddenly can't get my breath or swallow. I hear a man's voice of a particular timbre and have to sit down in my empty classroom to remind myself of where I am. Sometimes just sitting next to a tall man on a church pew can scare me. The flashbacks last only seconds, but I am, every time, aware of darkness, suffocation, weight and the knowledge that I can neither scream for help nor run away. Every day I have to think about who I am right now, where I am and what I'm doing at this moment. I have to work at living in the now. I don't dare drink alcohol. I have no idea what might happen to me unguarded.

We chat freely about our alters, about how other people seem to see us, how the effects of incest continue to haunt us, our goals for ourselves, our horror and outrage. I begin to feel faint glimmerings of a call to do what I can to stop this terrible plague of incestuous abuse, to protect children, to raise public awareness and to find my way out of the quicksand-filled swamp I'm walking in myself. I see how much work I still have to do on myself. It makes me angry.

Finally, the leader announces, "Loose ends." We each have an opportunity to make a further comment on the topic, to add a thought that may have just come to us, to express an insight or ask a question. We have a last "check-out." How am I feeling now? I generally answer, "Okay." Sometimes I can barely drive home I am so full of feeling, or alive with memories, or wanting to scream about the unfairness of it all. At times, I do scream in the car barreling down the highway at sixty miles per hour.

Of course, I have thought about suicide many times. Once, I sit in my car at the end of a parking area in Winton Woods trying to figure out if I can get up enough speed to kill myself by running into the huge oak tree on the other end. I am driving a Volvo and determine I'll probably just get hurt.

Anyway, I know insurance won't pay out to the children if I do that. Leaving my children high and dry is a concept I cannot entertain. I may not be a perfect parent, but I know my death would devastate my children. No matter how bad it is, I have made a decision to live as a baby, and I will stick to it now. My doctor informs me that even if I take all my antidepressants at once I'll only get sick and be put on suicide watch at the hospital. "You don't want that," he says. His description sounds worse than death to me. I am afraid he might be right. Looks like I'll be alive a while longer. I have to admit the discoveries I am making every day have caught my interest. The unfolding drama of my hitherto "regular" life captures my attention.

Therapist David is not good on the spiritual issues. Having been seriously connected to the church for my entire life, I have taken some things for granted which were now in question. I begin to read Psalm 94:12a "Blessed is the man whom thou dost chasten, O Lord ..." in a new way, and start thinking God must really love me since I feel mighty chastened. It doesn't give me any comfort. Everything I learned at church and Sunday School becomes suspect. If God loves me so much, why did this happen? If God has been right there with me, as well-meaning souls have tried to say, how come God didn't do what any prudent adult in the state of Ohio is required to do by law—namely, stop the crime and call the police? What about this pie-in-the-sky, by-and-by jazz where everybody gets forgiven and goes to glory? Is my dad going to be in heaven? If he is, then I don't want to go there. How do I know Dad didn't repent at the last minute like Emperor Constantine is said to have done? If God loves everyone, then God has to love Dad and all the other perpetrators of evil. I don't like the implications. Perhaps I should consider a different religion. Pagans don't seem to have these conflicts. Some of the women in my group report that they are survivors of ritualistic abuse and witchcraft practices. I have to say I don't know much about this. I feel I should count my blessings in this arena as well as the physical abuse arena. I realize there's always somebody who has suffered more than I have and in ways I can't even imagine. I, at least, had a misguided degree of caring from my parents. They can't have done everything wrong because I've come this far. As one of the newspaper advice columnists once wrote, even a stopped clock is right twice a day.

None of this thinking is helping me to feel any better. I have a spirit and a soul that I can't seem to avoid. God occasionally has an errand for me to run or a message to deliver to someone. I can't ignore that, or it nags me until I do it. Therefore, I can't become an atheist. I still don't understand how a God who makes butterflies also makes dung beetles. Do I believe there is some purpose for evil and ugliness in the world? I don't know. Do I believe Jesus died for my sins? Sure. I just don't know why anybody would go to that much trouble and misery for me when I don't even care if I get to go to heaven or not. I have no clue what the big picture is, and I can't go digging around in theology and philosophy to figure out what the will of God might be. I have to live here, now, and get along as best I can.

All these questions are slowing down my progress toward being a whole person. Instead of answering my concerns, religion seems to raise even more. Do I stop going to church, then? No, not even for one Sunday. I look around for spiritual help—a physician of the soul. Our church has recently hired a young pastor as an associate. He has some experience—this is not his first church—and he appears to be intelligent. I like his sermons, and he doesn't seem to be overwhelmed with the job—yet. I make an appointment to see him, to check him out, to see if he's going to panic if I mention incest. I've had the unfortunate experience of having pastors who are less able to deal with my problem than I am. These people tell me stuff like "When we get to Heaven, we'll all get crowns of jewels—rubies, emeralds, diamonds—and we'll throw them at the feet of Jesus." What do I care about that? Why should God give me a bunch of jewelry God wants back? I don't want money. I want peace. I want to feel like a real person, to be respected and cared for as a human being. I have to start believing in my own humanity. I am fed up with being a dollbaby doing what somebody else wants me to do. I don't need a God who just gives me "stuff." Some of these folks tell me that I have a Father in heaven who is an ideal father. That may be correct, but who am I to say what an ideal father might be? We aren't talking about an earthly father who has a few faults—maybe a little tight with money, or loses patience once in a while, or plays too much golf. We're talking about an earthly father who violates babies and young girls, treats them as objects, then tosses them aside as unfit for anything or anybody. I have a father in heaven like that?? I hope not.

The new guy in the church office, Bob, checks out okay. He doesn't pretend to be an expert on all subjects. He is willing to talk about anything and try to match it up with contemporary religious thought. He will pray with me, if that's what I want, but it's seldom what I want. I can pray on my own time for all the good it appears to be doing. Pastor Bob gives me some reading assignments from time to time. I read all of the Psalms at his suggestion because he knows I write poetry. We talk about them at length.

The psalmists are an odd bunch. We have no indication that David of biblical fame wrote them all. Possibly he wrote some of them, and many are attributed to him, but that gives us no facts about who wrote them. Whoever wrote them, they have an emotional range that is amazing. The writers will be in pits of despair, then on mountaintops of joy. I am only familiar with the pits. I am willing to celebrate that God has made many good and beautiful things. I am no clearer on the notion of why God would do this.

Bob and I read Richard Foster's book, *Prayer*, together. I am so struck by what, in my opinion, is the author's naïvete that I initiate a correspondence with him. Foster makes every effort to help. He sends me letters and tapes. I still am not sure he really gets the picture, although I find many meaningful concepts in his book and message. I am beginning to catch on to the fact that I am not like other people. I am exceedingly intense, I probably think way too much and my spiritual needs and longings are over the top. Bob encourages me to go ahead and be who I seem to be becoming.

I take issue with the idea that Jesus has experienced everything we experience. I bring up childbirth frequently in this context. When did Jesus go through labor and delivery? When did Jesus have PMS and mood swings and cramps? Who broke his heart by refusing a date with him? If God is interested in details, where is He when I can't choose between Coke and Pepsi? Jesus may have been in every way like other men, but he's just not cuttin' it with me. I start relating better to his mother. Even though it isn't a Presbyterian or even Protestant emphasis, I get interested in Mary. At least she's a woman. Outside of Roman Catholic theology, I get very little information, but I start paying attention to Mary and to all the women of the Bible. The trouble is that these women are either being forgiven for being harlots or are holy to begin with. I am neither a harlot nor holy. Beyond the everyday stuff, I don't know what to ask to be forgiven for. I don't even hate my parents—I don't like them, I'm mad as hell at them—but I don't hate them.

As I remember details of my abuse, I become unable to take communion any more. "It's barbaric!" I grouse to Bob. "Only a bunch of men would think you can get strength by eating somebody's body. And besides, it's just another man trying to get his body in my mouth." I actually choke on bread and wine at communion. Bob says its all psychosomatic, and maybe he's right, but I rarely take communion even today. Once or twice I've been able to take communion from him, but otherwise, no.

There's plenty of incest and other inappropriate sexual behavior in the Bible, but not too much guidance about how to deal with it. Anyway, the perpetrators aren't reading scripture and are certainly not recognizing themselves in it if they happen to read it. The occasions when something like that happens always end up in the newspapers and places like Court TV.

Again and Still

Again and still
Little notes of praise and hope
Ooze into the world like Midwestern rain,
Not pelting nor, yet, straightforwardly and
With efficiency, watering,
But seeping, creeping, crawling grayly into the everyday.
Then depressing, as relentlessly they pound their way,
Permeating and informing all of life
Until deep in the heated recesses of being,
They transform into a glorious sunshine
Awash with miracles of love.
Jesus comes—again and still.

Eleven

Years are going by. I continue at my job, which uses most of my energy. I sometimes get foggy in the classroom as Nancy or one of the others comes along to "help" me. I catch myself not listening to what people, including my students, say. I just miss it. Usually nothing important results from it, but I know when I've slipped up. My students become more and more difficult to handle. Society is changing and there are more and more students with emotional problems, who come from non-traditional homes, who have mental health issues. I get a student who is very hard to manage. His parents are on the verge of divorce, largely because of this child. If we could physically control him at school, he would probably be better off, but his mother is in denial. She messes with his diet and his medications and interferes daily with our program, wanting a million exceptions to be made for her child. He is a "special" case. Mostly he is just a little hyperactive, spoiled rotten and lazy. He is a big kid and used to being allowed to do whatever he wants.

One day, after we've hired a special person to look after this one kid, he starts climbing on some furniture stored in a room off the classroom. He stumbles and puts a small cut on his forehead. We get him into a chair, and when the supervisor of the program walks in the room, I have my hand lightly on the back of the child's head. The supervisor goes ballistic in a subdued sort of way. That is, he is furious, but he is not making a scene in front of the student. The supervisor hauls the kid off to the nurse to have her look at the injury. She cleans it off and places a dot bandage, the size of a dime, on the spot. The child and the person hired to look after him confirm that he cut himself climbing on the furniture, and I wasn't even in the room.

Shortly thereafter, the supervisor calls me into his office and chews me out. This may result in disciplinary action, he tells me. I point out two things: I was not present when the child was injured and my hand on his head was a "grounding" technique our occupational therapist had recommended for calming children. I have to talk to the parent at my supervisor's request and tell her how sorry I am the child is hurt. This is, of course, pure bull. The mother is not at all upset, believes the child who tells her he hurt himself and thanks me for taking the time to call her. I do not do well with the situation. I am terrified of my supervisor. I never really forgive him for that, and walk on eggs for the next ten years.

I understand that we can be sued for harming a child, that I can lose my job and my certification to teach, but this is not a circumstance in which any of these results are likely. The situation is pure Linnie. She's been chased out from behind her rock and she has gone bananas. Everything terrifies me now. Nancy has to rescue me daily from the little bumps, slights, annoyances and pure accidents that come my way and upset little Linnie. Linnie cries a lot, but only in private. This is a step forward for me, however, because up to now, I didn't have any feelings. Now I've got them, but don't recognize them right away, and don't know what to do with them. As my school assistant says, I'm "living and learning" just like my students.

On an inservice day, I am at school attending a workshop on something related to diversity or race relations or some such topic. The leaders have divided us into small groups. I am with my group in a section of our ancient auditorium. Our school building is about ninety years old with an auditorium that probably seats three hundred people. It has a full stage about four feet above the audience, lights, curtains—the whole magilla. The seats are wooden folding seats bolted together in rows on a concrete floor. I am half-turned in my seat listening to the assistant supervisor of our program trying to lead the discussion topic we've been assigned. I make a comment that I am serious about and feel has been slighted in the presentation. To Linnie's shock and distress, the assistant supervisor makes a smart-aleck remark about my comment. It is exactly what Dad might have said—a complete discount of my intelligence and ability to discern the salient issues, and meant to be funny. The pit of my stomach drops. I lose all color in my face, and I am about to bolt, but I'm sitting next to the school nurse.

"Don't let him get to you," she mutters. "He doesn't know."

This is true. He has no idea how what he said affects me. Our staff has always joked around, made cynical, sarcastic remarks to all comers, and, in general, taken a light view. This is absolutely necessary to maintain any kind of sanity and to do the work we have to do. It's like undertakers making death jokes. Among ourselves, we say outrageous things and play mild jokes on each other, but we always "have each other's back." Our job requires that we support each other fully. Our success lies largely in our ability to function as a team. We even use the same phrases in speaking to the children—we "run the code" every time. A child who is in trouble in one classroom will meet with exactly the same response to the behavior in any other classroom. These kids need consistency, need structure, need to know precisely what consequences follow what actions. This demands a faculty that works together, so the assistant supervisor is merely doing everyday things here.

Because of my emotional state, mostly unknown to my colleagues, I clam up immediately in the group. I hear nothing else of what goes on. I focus my attention on the stage door and the corner of the curtain hanging from one of the huge windows. I sit there frozen for as long as it takes until somebody announces a break. When the group breaks up, I rush to my classroom, lock myself in and let Linnie cry. She cries for about ten minutes before there's a knock on the door. At first, I ignore it. The knock is a little more insistent. I know somebody wants to know what's wrong. Reluctantly, I open the door to the school nurse, let her in and close the door behind her. She hugs me. I cry more. This is the first time I've ever let anybody touch me at all when I'm upset. I have always dealt with my problems privately. I never even send food back to the kitchen or demand my money back when I'm brought the wrong thing in a restaurant. Nobody touches me. Linnie is desperate, though. She is not at home where she can barricade herself in her room. She actually has to get through the rest of the day with these people. I am thinking of going home "sick." This wouldn't exactly be a lie.

Bea, the nurse, takes it easy on me. She doesn't ask for explanations or give me any advice. Whatever Linnie does appears to be okay. This hasn't happened before. Usually I get advice as to what I'm supposed to feel and do. I am unaccustomed to having Linnie out in broad daylight. I barely recognize her myself. I'm ashamed of crying. Linnie and I both know crying's a lost cause. We understand that big girls accept whatever happens to them and show no response other than the expected smile when it's a positive situation.

Bea hangs on only as long as Linnie will let her—which isn't a really long time. I get a little more composed and tell Bea that I know Paul had no way of knowing how his comment would fall on my ears. I ask her to please tell him that I am not angry with him, that I understand that he is ignorant in the truest sense of the word of my status. I realize sexual abuse/incest is not an experience, like winning the lottery, where a person is likely to yell, "Guess what?! Guess what?! I was sexually abused by my dad!!" This is information I am ashamed of. I think that I am somehow to blame for my dad's behavior.

Actually, as I think back on it, Dad did blame me for the incest. I was too cute, it turns out, and just irresistible. As if I could do anything about that! I suppose those white cotton diapers just set off my pudgy little figure to a fare-thee-well. Oh, I was cute, all right. Now I feel embarrassed about having been a baby and a small child. It doesn't get better. Several months go by before I am able to tell Paul that I have long since forgiven him for a thoughtless comment, don't remember it any more and want to continue our friendship.

The shame of being a child continues to compound. My Aunt Margaret dies during the period of therapy and coming to terms with incest. When I go to her funeral, I meet some of her first husband's relatives. She had been widowed a number of years before she married my dad. I know some of these people, but others I've just heard of. When one woman is introduced to me, she has to think a minute to place me, but place me she does. "Oh, yes," she says. "I remember you. Your mother brought you out to our farm once when you were about two or three years old. You stepped in the mud by our pond, and my mother said, 'Why that nasty little girl!'" Then she laughed. My cousin, J, suggested that she and I go into another room, and I couldn't have been more relieved. Now I think I am responsible for being a three-year-old with muddy shoes.

Nobody appears to remember anything positive about my childhood, including me. I believe that I really am a nasty little girl. I know all too well the things I do and I am pretty sure most of them are nasty. I have allergies that break out my hands in eczema and make my nose run. I have to deal with this. I have to use the toilet every day, and this is an embarrassment. I am forty-five years old before I can feel okay about going into a ladies' room. Sometimes years go by between visits to the doctor. I just live through whatever happens. Nancy is raising my children. She takes them to the doctor whenever they need to go. They are all right with doctor visits and whatever procedures need to be done. They are not thrilled about getting booster shots and what-not, but they take it in stride. They are normal.

As a small child, my daughter Karen got a cut over her eye that needed stitches. I took her to the doctor, and she cried as though some limb were being removed sans anesthesia. She shouted for her Daddy.

"Do you think that if Daddy were here, maybe this wouldn't be happening?" I asked her.

"Yes," she answered.

Karen saw her father as a protector, someone who loved

her so much he would do anything to make her happy and comfortable. She had every reason to think this. I am glad she felt this way, but it is completely foreign to me. When I broke my leg, my dad was aggravated that he had to take me to the hospital to get the "damned" thing set.

As I get further along in my journey toward wholeness, I am blessed with some good friends who, while they haven't been down this particular road, are willing to accompany me. I begin to learn to share with them over time and to trust them with myself. I am still not much of a hugger and toucher. I still require long periods of time alone.

One problem I've had to grapple with concerns relationships with men. For quite a while after I divorced H, I thought I needed a man in my life. Some women feel that they do, but I believe, now, that I am not likely one of them. I enjoy my freedom so much! I never want to have to consider another person's schedule or needs again on a daily basis. It has taken some time to accept the fact that I am probably never again going to have a sexual relationship. I say " probably" just to hedge my bet. I am not even looking, which enables me to be friends with some men, regardless of age, and to spend time doing mainly what I want to do. I have told friends that I'd be happy to remarry as long as the man in question lives somewhere else and doesn't need to see me more than once a week tops. I like men. I don't like having to deal with anyone all day and all night. I like quiet. I don't even watch TV every day. My daughter, Laura, usually phones if there's anything on the news she thinks I should know about. That doesn't even happen every day.

My experience with men is, I think, forever marked, and ruined by one man whom I know from Mensa. I join Mensa because I am looking to develop some new friends. I think that I will meet people who have similar interests, and anyway, I am ready to enjoy something about myself: I qualify for Mensa membership! Mensa requires proof that a person has an IQ in the top two percent of the population. This man I meet is a person I have originally met when Herb is interim pastor of the man's church. The man—I'll call him "Jack"—has a wife and family, and a strong involvement with Mensa. Once I join Mensa, Jack is all over me. He gropes. He dances way too close. He wants to leave together from Mensa events, particularly the wedding reception of another member's daughter. I avoid him as much as I can. The really bad thing occurs three days before my own daughter's wedding.

Jack is living out of Cincinnati at that time, but has to come to court here to divorce his wife. I suppose she finally has had enough of his dreadful behavior. At any rate, he calls and wants to come over for pizza at my house before going back home. I don't want him to do this, but Linnie has trouble being assertive. My younger daughter is home, so I think I'll be all right. I am so wrong!

When Jack arrives, I suggest we go out for the pizza. He won't hear of it. I suggest going out to a couple of different places, but he insists on calling for pizza. No sooner has the pizza been consumed, than he rapes me in my own living room. My daughter has just gone out with her friends. I am too scared to fight, but I keep saying no over and over. I manage to keep him from actually penetrating me, but the violation is there all the same. As fast as possible, I get him out of there. Of course, I should have run next door and called the police. I should have left with my daughter. I should have done any number of things to prevent the attack, but in my child alter, I could do none of those things. When I enter an alter personality, the adult part of me often knows what is going on and what to do about it, but she is simply observing from a distance. It is like watching a horror movie.

My first response, after locking the door, is to get in the shower. I scrub myself raw trying to get Jack off me, but it isn't anything physical that can be removed. My soul has been ripped up and tossed out like a candy wrapper. I feel like a piece of candy—quickly dispatched and forgotten. A non-essential bit of frivolity in an ugly world.

I try to read—my usual escape from reality—but I can't focus. Finally, I call my girlfriend, Jackie, who is also a survivor of incest, and she simply tells me where to meet her. I am really not sure how I drive to the restaurant we've agreed on, but I get there, and she is sitting in her car. The restaurant is closed, so she puts me in her car where I bawl for quite a while.

"It's not your fault," she tells me as many times as it takes—and it takes a lot.

I always think it's my fault. I should have put up a bigger fight, ordered him off my property, called the cops, kicked his ass—all those things I am sure I can do when I'm watching TV. I believe I'm not smart enough, tough enough. I hardly realize, even though Jackie is telling me this, that I am Linnie. Tank Girl has taken cover, as usual. Nancy is not feeling anything, and Ted has, apparently, taken a hike. I am slowly learning that it can take a very long time to recognize one's defense systems, but only seconds to activate them. I feel I'm in the midst of a cold war where the big red button can be pushed by anybody. I am helpless in the face of my own defense mechanisms. They just take me over whenever they think it's appropriate. My whole life seems meaningless in the wake of this one incident. I suddenly can't remember anything I ever did right, but I've somehow got to get hold of myself.

I am still seeing the therapist, still attending group meetings, still meeting with my pastor, but I don't think I can bring myself to discuss this latest development in any of those places. I feel so stupid! How can an adult woman with the kind of responsibilities I have allow a thing like that rape to happen? What am I going to do now?

I hear that Jack is going to some Mensa convention or something in San Francisco. Before that happens, my son comes home for his sister's wedding. I decide to take TV action. I will ask my son to get some of his friends together and beat Jack up when he gets to San Francisco. Fortunately, my son has more brains than I do. We have a wonderful time hashing out the plot of this beating, planning strategy, trying to think of the legal problems that could occur. We discuss timing, how the guys are going to know Jack and everything. It's worthy of "City Confidential" or one of those other true crime shows. In the end, nothing happens. The guys don't even try it, which I am happy about. I am embarrassed by my anger, by my desire for revenge, by my flair for the dramatic. It is a step forward, though. My children are beginning to get an idea of what makes their mother tick.

Up to this point, the children are simply aware that I have experienced abuse. I have asked them repeatedly if they remember anything in their own childhoods that is suspect. They do not. Now I worry that I have warped them somehow by my own efforts at survival. What have I taught them about relationships? They are all grown and whatever damage I've done is done. They seem to be okay. They have their own problems, but, on the whole, they seem to be all right. I have said for years that I was hoping they'd be "creatively unadjusted," and I think I've succeeded. Each child is his or her own person, and they have a closeness to each other that amazes me. They actually talk to me, too, but they don't want to talk about child abuse—it upsets them. I'm fine with that. I don't want to cause them any pain because they are my main lifeline.

I take to wearing turtles as a symbol of my progress. A friend gave me a small one as a gift for taking care of her cat while she was away. She said, "It takes a long time to deal with abuse, but the turtle will help you hang in there. It was the tortoise who won the race." I have a collection of turtle jewelry, I have worn turtle stickers, and I have several turtle models: the original gift, a soapstone carving, a pottery dish and a couple of others. I adopt Eeyore, the donkey from *Winnie the Pooh*, as my mascot. "Gloomy old Eeyore" with his negative attitude is accepted and loved by his friends. I feel I've been accepted, too, after all these years.

The most significant change I've made is my name. Linde Grace White is not the name I was given at birth. When I felt I had made enough progress to warrant calling myself a "new creation," I legally changed my name. I had my birth certificate changed as well as everything else. I enjoyed choosing my name. Linde is Scandinavian (totally unrelated to my ethnic background). It means a serpent, which is a symbol for wisdom. I have certainly gained wisdom. Grace is for the grace of God, without which I could have never made this journey. White is my maternal grandmother's birth name. I wanted to keep some connection to my family of origin because I love them, but I didn't want the connection to be too direct. Also, my birth name is distinctive and I like the relative anonymity of "White."

My Progress

I seem to be walking in chewing gum
Half-melted on the pavement,
Sticking to my shoes and
Pulling up in thin adhesive strings.
Progress is wretchedly slow,
And I'm leaving a disgusting trail
Behind with every labored step—
And, what's worse, it isn't even my gum.

Occasionally, now, I can express feelings. Sometimes they come as a bit of a shock to me. A friend died about two years ago. She was not a person I was particularly close to, although I liked her, had worked with her on church projects and enjoyed her company. I was struck by how deeply I felt her death. She was ten years or so older than I, so I don't think my reaction was to the idea that somebody my own age had died. Furthermore, she had had cancer for a while, so her death was not unexpected. I took a day off work to attend her funeral. It was lovely, as funerals go. I did not cry then, but I did later in the day, remembering happy times with my friend. I couldn't understand what was going on with me until I asked another friend. Grief! That's what it was. Okay. Now I know what happens when I grieve.

I have learned a lot about joy from being a grandmother. I am hopelessly in love with my two grandsons. I watched both of them being born and felt an instant bond with them. Seeing them grow and progress is the happiness of my life. They are always good for a laugh, and I can allow myself to be "cuddled" by the boys. It is easier to relate to them than it was to my own children when they were little. Then, I raised them (or maybe I should say, Nancy raised them) by the book. The book said to hold them. I held them. The book said to encourage them to express themselves, but to have structure and rules for them. I did it. I related to them well, I think, because I wanted their lives to be so different from mine. I was always surprised when they wanted to talk with me about serious topics, astounded when they asked my advice and thrilled when they agreed with some plan I proposed. That sort of thing comes more naturally, now, with my grandchildren. It also helps not to be responsible for them all the time, too. I can take them places or spend time with them, but they go back to their parents shortly.

Short periods of time—that's the key to my relationships these days. I love my family and friends deeply, but I can only handle being with people for relatively brief times. I can host Thanksgiving dinner or attend a Christmas Day celebration without a problem. I can even handle a weekend visit somewhere, as long as I don't have to entertain or be entertained constantly. My Myers-Briggs type has consistently indicated "introvert" for my entire adult life. One of the best vacations of my life was a week I spent with my cousin in California. She worked all day almost every day. I had several days to explore the area driving her car around. She was working with a Girl Scout Day Camp, so I tagged along on their trip to the beach, but, mostly I was on my own throughout the day. I visited the places I wanted to see. I love to get together with friends or family two or three times a week, but I don't like lengthy phone conversations. Perhaps some of this will change now that I have retired from teaching and will be less emotionally drained on a daily basis.

I see my abuse today like a terrible mistake in a beautiful

painting. It has changed the entire picture forever, yet it is part of the picture and informs the picture, giving it a certain direction and organization. When a painter makes an error, he or she "paints it out" or incorporates the error into the finished picture. The error is actually still there, yet it is not the first thing we notice about the picture.

Another way I look at incest is the way I might experience a beautiful damask napkin that has been indelibly stained. The stain goes all the way through the fabric, yet the piece is still usable. I could dye the piece to cover the stain, but the stain remains there. The stain drives the way I use the napkin, and I have choices. I can throw the whole thing away and lose much that is valuable. I can scrub the floors with it or clean my paintbrush on it, but that is unworthy of an otherwise fine article. I can choose to work with the stain, to work the stain into the design somehow, to proudly use the item for its intended purpose.

I am not willing to let incest become my self. A friend who has cancer says, "I am not cancer. I am a person with cancer." I am not a victim, I am a person whose life has been forever altered by incest, but I choose to let that life be purposeful, usable—to be a life that brings joy to me and to others. I want my life to shine as an example to others, to raise awareness of the problem of incest and sexual abuse, to stop it in whatever ways I can and to say to other survivors: You do not have to be a victim. You can succeed in being your own person. If I can do it, so can you.

Even after all I've done to move toward wholeness and humanity, to accept myself as a worthy individual and to make my life count, I still feel, at times, like the alters I was forced to develop to take care of me as a child. The alters, I like to think, are honorably retired. They are on permanent vacation in a happy place. If I had to, in an emergency, I could call on them to help me out, but I really can handle life on my own now. I am able to recognize situations and respond appropriately these days.

I had to have some surgery in recent years, and in one case, I knew that I probably was not going to like the preparation beforehand. In the past, I would have stewed, worried, and gotten myself into a swivet—or Nancy, whichever happened first. This time, I was able to tell my doctor exactly what bothered me and what scared me about the hospital stay. We discussed how to handle the problems, and he was most careful to understand whether or not Nancy, Linnie or Ted had objections to what was happening. On surgery day, I was fully present, a little nervous, but well able to handle it. I had no trouble at all, and recovered without incident. I am still no fan of medical procedures. I still have to take a small dose of antidepressant since my physician is sure my brain is no longer making sufficient chemicals to keep me on an even keel. This, however, is a far cry from being drugged up, dependent on alcohol, unemployed or a lot of other ugly things I can think of. I do what needs to be done for my health like any responsible adult.

Spiritual issues continue to be a concern. I consider myself to be a Christian, but in no way a fundamentalist. I have a high tolerance for other expressions of spiritual life, and I think that incest and sexual abuse survivors are especially vulnerable to religious doubts, fears and uncertainty. I am learning to accept my uncertainty and doubts as part of my expression of faith. I believe it is a mistake to ignore the spiritual aspect of oneself; however, survivors are deeply wounded in this area, so they have to struggle, grieve and come to terms with a personal expression of this part of personhood. I have had to discount a fair amount of traditional Christian doctrine for my own sanity. As I said, I am unable to take communion except on rare occasions when I can reduce it in my mind to something light and not serious. The words, "This is my body," just send a shudder through me. I am overwhelmed by the barbarity of the idea that consuming somebody's flesh is going to make me strong or more like that person. I know that is a primitive notion from centuries ago, but, more to the point, communion represents to me the attempt of yet another man to get his body in my mouth. I feel mainly revulsion, regardless of the true symbolism of it. As an Elder in my church, I can "dish it out," but I can't take it. I understand that for others, communion is profoundly meaningful in a positive sense, but it's not for me. I say if Jesus really wants to feed me, he'll take me out for burgers and fries.

It is hard to rid myself of the idea that I'm worthless. My entire life seems to be a string of criticisms and improvement projects. I can hear my parents, even as I write this, whispering that I really am no good, that I have a long way to go. I find the church to be no help at all here. Much of Christian doctrine revolves around the mistaken thought that people are unworthy of the sacrifice of Jesus. It is difficult for me to reconcile John 3:16 with everything I was taught in the church. It seems we can't win for losing. It is much easier for me to identify with the apostle Paul: "Wretched man that I am! Who will deliver me from this body of death?" (Rom. 7:24).

The second I develop some self-esteem, I get shot down for being "proud." If I say I have no sin, I'm a liar—read it in the Bible. My righteousness is "as filthy rags." I imagine I will continue to have these issues for the rest of my life. The way I deal with this is to simply ignore the old voices in my head.

I remind myself of where they're coming from, and I try to keep the real accomplishments in front of me. I journal and record the good things along with the bad. Here's a sample from February 4, 1997:

> Survived the day, but don't feel good. The nicest thing happened! __________ called to say she'd been thinking about me, she misses me and I'm one of her favorite people! Now, could anything be more golden? When I think nobody cares, I can come back to today. What an honor and privilege it is to have people who support you! It certainly motivates me to try even harder.

The lady who called me is an older woman in my church, and just phoned for that reason only. I try to remember that even little things I say or do from my own limited experience can have as profound an effect on others as that message had on me.

Writing, for me, has been a part of the solution to my own life dilemma. It has helped me clarify and think through issues. I don't believe I am ever going to be a happy little nincompoop. I am not going to have a mansion with servants, my own jet, a personal assistant, endless joy and peace—well, not in this life, at least. I am probably not going to bring about world peace, be elected President or sing my heart out at Lincoln Center or Carnegie Hall. Yet, if I have prevented one child from suffering abuse, helped one adult overcome the problems facing him or her or made one perpetrator stop and think for a second, I think I will feel validated in my efforts.

Linen

A white damask napkin,
Vines and roses embossed
White on white, richly, thickly,
Edged in neat, straight stitches,
Lies in a drawer, unused.
I slowly unfold and study
What is there to see: tightly woven,
Intricate, deep design, and
Darkly stained, completely through.

About the Author

Linde Grace White has become not merely a survivor, but a thriver in the wake of childhood sexual abuse. After years of therapy, participation in survivor groups, extensive reading and spiritual counseling, Linde Grace emerged.

Always a writer (from age eight), she has written poetry and stories in her spare time. A number of her works have been published in magazines and smaller publications. She has won Honorable Mention in the *Writer's Digest* Poetry Competition and other awards.

Linde Grace earned a B.A. in English from the University of Louisville and a M.Ed. in guidance and counseling from Xavier University.

In addition to raising three children to successful adulthood, she taught emotionally disturbed/behavior disordered children for more than twenty years in a special education program of the Hamilton County Educational Service Center in Ohio. Most of these children have a history of abuse. She retired from teaching in June 2004.

Linde Grace is a member of VOICES in Action, Inc. and the International Women's Writing Guild. She is an Elder in the Pleasant Ridge Presbyterian Church in Cincinnati, Ohio.